NORTH CAROLINA

CHILD RELOCATION LAW

LEE ROSEN | LISA ANGEL

Morgan and Dawson
Publishing

Lee Rosen & Lisa Angel/Morgan & Dawson Publishing
4101 Lake Boone Trail
Raleigh, NC 27607
MorganandDawson.com

Lisa Angel
Board Certified Family Law Specialist
angel@rosen.com

Lee Rosen
Rosen Law Firm
rosen@rosen.com

Ordering Information:
Quantity sales. Special discounts are available on quantity purchases by corporations, associations, and others. For details, contact the Morgan & Dawson Publishing at publisher@morgananddawson.com

North Carolina Child Relocation Law/ Lee Rosen & Lisa Angel. —1st ed.
ISBN: 978-0-9993-5200-7 (print)

TABLE OF CONTENTS

WHY WE WROTE
THE BOOK ON RELOCATION

Sharing custody of children is perhaps one of the most difficult endeavors parents face. Regardless of whether parents share time equally or one parent has significantly more time than the other, parenting children in separate households is stressful and often emotionally draining. It's hard enough to raise children when parents live together. When a breakup, formal separation, or divorce creates two separate households, the challenge can seem insurmountable.

Now consider those two households, which may have radically different parenting styles, and add in that one parent needs or wants to move out of state. The stress meter just hit 1,000!

This book addresses many scenarios that could lead to a parent's move and outlines how to deal with these types of situations if they arise.

Moving is not always a choice. Jobs and life events sometimes require one parent to move.

Custody arrangements, whether court ordered or agreed, are difficult to change. That's especially true if the change results in one parent living several states away from his or her child.

As a parent, you need to know your legal options when a potential out-of-state move is under consideration. As with most child custody issues, there are plenty of myths out there. If you know the law relating to the relocation of children, you'll be in a better position to understand and evaluate the options you have.

Unfortunately, no single rule in North Carolina governs the relocation of children after a custody order or agreement is entered. This book aims to help you navigate these difficult situations.

WHAT YOU NEED TO KNOW
ABOUT CHILD CUSTODY
DETERMINATION AND MODIFICATION

"Legal custody," "physical custody," "joint custody," "primary custody," and "substantial change of circumstances": you hear these terms all the time. You know they relate to child custody laws in North Carolina.

But what do these terms mean, and how do they apply to you and your child custody case? Let's consider an example.

Note: You may notice that throughout this book, we interchangeably use examples involving a single child and examples with multiple children. The number of children in a family makes no difference in the application of child custody laws. Anywhere that you read an example about a single child, that principle applies equally to multiple children, and vice versa.

Child Custody Generally

Our couple, Don and Danielle, have been married for nine years and have two children, ages seven and four. Unfortunately, Don and Danielle have drifted apart over the past four years. They argue all the time, they never get along, and they cannot stand each other's company. Don and Danielle have tried marriage counseling for the past five months, but it isn't helping. They decide that it is best for their marriage, best for each of them individually, and best for their kids if they separate. Don moves out of the family home and into an apartment about 10 miles away from the house where Danielle continues living with the children.

Don works full time as a consultant and often travels during the workweek, sometimes within North Carolina and sometimes nationally. Danielle also works full time at a local branch of a major bank.

Both Don and Danielle are great parents. They are both very involved with their children, and each would say the same about the other.

The Best Interests of the Children

Don and Danielle both hire attorneys to represent them as they divide and distribute the marital property, determine alimony and child support, and work out a child custody arrangement. They participate in mediation to reach a settlement.

While in mediation, their goal is to negotiate a custody arrangement and schedule that serves the best interests of their children. This arrangement will not necessarily be what is best for either Don or for Danielle as individuals.

This is the prevailing legal standard—and the guidepost for both parents and the court—for all child custody cases. What is in the "*best interests*" of the child or children involved?

Four common child custody factors help the court decide what is in the best interests of the child:

1. the child's age,

2. the stability of each parent,

3. the schedule and work obligations of each parent, and

4. the willingness of each parent to involve the other parent in visits with the child and events in the child's life.

Court Order or Separation Agreement?

Don and Danielle successfully reach an out-of-court settlement in mediation. They then decide to formalize that child custody agreement and the agreed terms of child support in a consent court order.

Even though they both agreed to the custody arrangement, Don and Danielle, on the advice of their lawyers, thought it best to have their agreement incorporated into a court order. If problems do come up, an official court order can better protect each of them and can make it easier to modify the custody arrangement. With a court order, the parents can turn to the court when they have a conflict.

If the custody provisions remain in the form of a separation agreement rather than a court order, Don and Danielle wouldn't have involved a court to help them resolve disputes. Generally, then, they would have to work together to negotiate any modifications to the custody arrangement. That process can be difficult unless both parents agree to the modification. Therefore, disputes can be harder to resolve with an agreement.

Legal Custody

Don and Danielle agree to joint legal custody.

Legal custody means the right to make major decisions involving the child. In other words, a parent who has legal custody has the right—and the responsibility—to make important decisions in the child's life. These decisions may include the following:

- where the child will attend school,
- how the child will be disciplined,
- whether the child will have braces,
- whether the child should undergo surgery or other major medical treatment, or
- what doctor or medical facility will treat the child.

Joint Legal Custody

Don and Danielle, like most parents, have agreed to *joint legal custody*.

"Joint" simply means that they equally share these legal decisions. This means that Don and Danielle must consult with each other on all major decisions involving the kids. They have to reach a mutual agreement on every decision; neither parent can "pull rank" with joint legal custody.

Don and Danielle know that all major decisions that come up from now until both of their kids turn 18 will need to be made together, with the best interests of the kids as the primary concern.

Physical Custody

Along with joint legal custody, Don and Danielle also agree to share *physical custody*. Physical custody refers to where the children will live on a day-to-day basis.

Don and Danielle agree that their kids will live with Danielle from Monday to Thursday every week. They will live with Don every other Thursday through Monday; on the off weeks, they will stay with Danielle.

Don and Danielle also agree that when Don is in town, he will have weekday visitation one afternoon and evening each week. Finally, they agree to divide visitation on all holidays in half. They both agree that this schedule is in the best interests of both of their kids.

Because Danielle has the children more than Don does, she is considered to have primary physical custody. This doesn't mean that her time with the kids is more important than Don's time or that Don has less of a say in how the children are raised. Both parents are actively involved and can maintain strong relationships with their kids. Primary physical custody only means that due to everyone's schedules, the children spend more time living in Danielle's home.

The Terminology Is Not Everything

Sometimes parents involved in a custody dispute get bogged down in the unfamiliar legal terminology. Thankfully, Don and Danielle quickly learned not to focus on the labels of "joint physical custody" or "primary physical custody."

They realized that what mattered was developing a schedule that would allow each parent adequate time with the kids, within their own work schedules and availability.

Day-to-day decisions are made by whichever parent the kids are with on that day. So, when Don has the kids, he gets to make decisions like these:

1. what to feed them for meals;

2. what time they go to bed;

3. whether they can visit at a friend's house;

4. what clothes they wear; and

5. what, if any, TV they can watch or video games they can play.

Don and Danielle recognize that they can make these day-to-day decisions independently of the other parent. For the sake of the kids, though, they agree to create an overall routine and schedule that both will follow as closely as possible.

Modification of a Custodial Arrangement

There are many reasons why a parent might need to modify a child custody arrangement. These reasons might include the following:

1. one parent has to move to another home or even another area,

2. a parent's work schedule changes,

3. one parent is not exercising his or her custodial periods under the current custody order or agreement,

4. the child's schedule changes,

5. a child's preference changes (in some instances),

6. the child's safety is at risk, or

7. the child's stability is at risk.

Modifying a Court Order Versus a Separation Agreement

In any situation, modifying the terms of custody requires that there be a *substantial change in circumstances*. To be considered substantial, such a change must affect the child's well-being.

If a court order is in place, the court must be involved in any changes. On the other hand, when a separation agreement specifies the custody arrangement, both parents must agree to the change. Together they must rewrite that portion of their separation agreement into a new contract or amendment.

So, how does modifying a custody arrangement actually work, particularly when it involves a relocation? Let's explore a few examples of when the parents would and would not need to modify their court order or separation agreement.

When a Custody Order is in Place

When a custody order is in place, it is an official court order. That means that a parent must file a motion to modify the order, and a judge must allow the motion before a new custody arrangement can be made.

If One Parent Has to Relocate and Plans to Take the Children

Fast forward a few years: Don and Danielle have now been divorced for four years. Their kids are twelve and nine. The consent custody order based on their agreement from mediation is still in place. Although both Don and Danielle agree that it has been difficult at times, they have followed all the agreed terms. The children seem to be doing quite well despite the divorce.

However, now Danielle has received a promotion with her job at the bank that will require her to move halfway across the country.

The new job comes with a significant pay raise and the assurance that she will not have to travel for work. She will be moving to an area with one of the best public school districts in the country. Plus, it happens in be in the county where she grew up, and her parents and siblings live within an hour's drive.

The existing custody order, specifying that Danielle and Don share physical custody and giving Don the opportunity to see the kids one afternoon and evening every week that he's in town, simply won't work anymore. And Don cannot keep the kids regularly since he travels so much for work.

Does this count as a substantial change in circumstances so that Danielle can ask the court to modify the custody order?

There Is a Substantial Change of Circumstances

Yes, this type of cross-country move does represent a substantial change of circumstances. Therefore, Danielle files a motion asking the court to modify their consent order. The judge grants Danielle's motion and schedules a hearing. Eventually, after listening to both sides, the court modifies the consent order because there is a substantial change in circumstances affecting the children's well-being.

Because the Relocation Would Benefit the Children

Even though Danielle will be taking the kids farther away from their father, she has shown that the move would be advantageous to the kids. She has explained the benefits for the kids: a great school district, extended family nearby, plus Danielle's improved job. That higher income, combined with an assurance of no travel, will enable Danielle to better provide for the children, financially and otherwise.

In this example, it would be detrimental for the kids to live with Don, even though they would be staying where they have lived all of their lives. With his work schedule, Don could not ensure that he would be available every day to maintain a home for the kids. An absent parent can't effectively look after children, help with homework, attend school and sporting events, and so on.

Living with a parent who is often absent would not benefit the children at all.

An Example of When There Is No Substantial Change of Circumstances

Now consider the same facts, but this time Danielle's promotion only requires her to move about an hour away. The school district is no different, and no extended family lives in this new location.

Again, Danielle plans to take the children with her. Don still sometimes travels during the week and simply does not have the availability to properly and adequately spend time with the children.

Now that there will be a one-hour drive between Danielle's new residence and Don's residence, it will be difficult to transfer the kids every other Thursday and one afternoon and evening during the week. That schedule would subject the kids to frequent hour-long trips each way to Don's home and then to return to Danielle's. With traffic and their extracurricular activities, this could be tricky to manage.

Danielle again filed the motion to modify the custody order, but the judge denied it. The custody schedule must remain the same.

No Negative Impact on the Children

This time, the judge denied the motion to modify because there was no evidence that Don and Danielle's kids would be negatively affected by moving one hour away.

Note that this time, there was no evidence that such a relocation would affect or could affect the kids' school performance, grades, or participation in extracurricular activities.

Yes, the additional travel time will be time-consuming and expensive for each parent. But that inconvenience does not negatively affect the welfare of the kids.

Life Changes Do Not Automatically Mean a Modification is Needed
As this example shows, every change in the lives of the parents or the children does not lead to the automatic modification of a custody order. The parents must show something more.

Specifically, a parent requesting a modification must show that the change will be advantageous to the child's well-being. A parent trying to block a modification request can show either that the proposed change would harm the children or that it would simply have no impact.

When a Separation Agreement is in Place

As you've seen, parents who want or need to modify a custody order must file a motion in court. But what about parents whose custody provisions are in a separation agreement?

When a separation agreement, rather than a court order, specifies custody provisions, the parents do not have to file anything. These parents have more flexibility in how they change the agreement.

This is because the separation agreement is a contract that both parties entered voluntarily. The court was not involved in the execution of the agreement.

Returning to Don and Danielle, imagine that they had left their custody provisions in a separation agreement instead of obtaining a court order. Now how would Danielle go about modifying the terms if she has to relocate?

Modification Options

Parents with a separation agreement detailing custody have three options to modify the custodial schedule. They can:

1. negotiate with the other parent for a change,

2. return to mediation to try to reach another agreement, or

3. file a custody action in court.

Negotiate with the Other Parent

Since both parents voluntarily entered the separation agreement, Danielle would have to obtain Don's consent to modify the terms. She would need to start by explaining the change in her life and discussing her proposed modification with Don.

If they agreed on what the new terms would be, then either of them or a lawyer could draft an amendment to the separation agreement. The new agreement would need to be signed in front of a notary to be legally binding. At that point, it would replace the old custody provisions.

Return to Mediation

If Danielle has to move out of state and wants to take the children with her, Don is not likely to agree to that new custody arrangement.

Where a simple discussion or negotiation doesn't work, parents can return to mediation. Engaging a third-party mediator trained in dispute resolution may help them develop a new custodial schedule. Returning to mediation would allow Don and Danielle to retain control over the custodial decisions. It would also help them avoid the cost of a court battle.

Some separation agreements require the parties to try to mediate future custodial disputes before resorting to litigation.

File a Custody Action in Court

Suppose Don and Danielle tried to negotiate the custody change on their own and failed. Then they tried mediation, only to fail again. Now Danielle, as the parent seeking the change in custody, will have to file a custody action against Don in court.

This is the last resort, after all other avenues to reach a new agreement have failed.

The court would treat Danielle's case as a new custody action. Both parents would be required to complete the court-ordered custody mediation before they could get a court date in front of a judge.

The judge would hear all the evidence and decide on a new custody schedule that he or she believes is in the best interests of the kids. This custody schedule would then be written as a court order. The court order would override the custody terms in the separation agreement.

Hopefully, Don and Danielle's example has explained some common terms and legal standards. Of course, everything is harder when it's your own family that's breaking up. Often people become overwhelmed and can't figure out where to start. So what should you do first when faced with a major life change like a relocation? Our next chapter will help you decide.

RELOCATION:
WHAT DO I DO FIRST?

It took six years, but you finally did it. You got the job in management. In a month, you'll move to Seattle. You thought this day would never come!

But Seattle is a long way from Raleigh, North Carolina. What are you going to do about the children? You don't have much time before you need to move.

Of course, you want them to move with you. You never really let yourself think about whether they would stay in North Carolina. Would a judge force you to leave them behind and give their father full custody?

Moving out of state for any reason almost always creates issues with custody arrangements, including the time and additional expense of travel.

Regardless of whether a court order or settlement agreement is in place regarding custody, or even if you have no formal agreement at all, things just got a lot more complicated. Needless to say, driving 15 minutes to pick up your children is much simpler than flying across the country to see them.

So what happens when one parent needs to move out of state? What do you do first?

The answers will vary depending on whether you have a custody agreement and, if so, what type it is.

Whether your custody arrangement was established through a separation agreement or by a custody order from the court, you must follow its terms. Unless that arrangement addresses your move out of state, moving would probably violate the agreement or order. You will have to have the arrangement modified, either by consent of the other parent for an agreement or by a judge if you have a court order regarding custody.

What If a Custody Order is in Place?

For example, let's say you share 50/50 custody with your ex-husband under a court-entered custody order. The children attend school close to your neighborhood. Both of you share responsibilities for the children's school and social activities. You tell your ex-husband about your new job and ask whether he agrees that the children should move with you to Seattle. He says absolutely not.

Should you move first and contact a lawyer to modify custody after you are in Seattle? What if you file the motion before you leave but move with the children before the court hearing?

Regardless of whether the order specifically prohibits moving out of state without the other party's consent or a modification of the order, it will be impossible to abide by the current order. You can't be in two places at once, so you'll violate the order if you move.

If that happens, the other parent could file a motion for contempt for violating the order and ask that you immediately return the children to North Carolina. It may even be possible for the other parent to gain temporary custody and the immediate return of the children to North Carolina if you violate the order.

What If the Other Parent Had Only Minimal Visitation?

Staying with this example, let's change the facts. Now the children's dad only has visitation every other weekend, on half the holidays, and for two weeks in the summer. The order is silent on either of you moving out of state.

Technically, you could move with the children and still follow the order. You would just need to fly the children back for visits every other weekend, half of the holidays, and two weeks in the summer.

In this example, because the order doesn't specifically forbid you from moving out of state and visits could continue uninterrupted, you could move without violating the order, at least in theory.

That said, it's still not a good idea to make a drastic cross-country move without first addressing custody. Yes, in a technical sense, you could follow the order if you could afford to fly the children back every other weekend. But the children would still be uprooted from their current life, plus they would now spend a minimum of several hours every other weekend traveling.

Even if the distance were much shorter, such as a neighboring state only four or five hours away by car, you would be changing in the children's lives substantially. While the travel would not be nearly as burdensome as cross-country flights, the kids would be uprooted from school and friends. Their lives would definitely be disrupted.

Thus, the need to address custody is still there. Moving without amending the agreement or the order has the potential to create much bigger problems.

Note that under these examples, if the court order did include a provision restricting out-of-state moves, you would violate the order by moving without first modifying it. This is so even in the example where your ex-husband only has minimal visitation.

What Do You Risk If the Custody Order is not Modified Before You Move?

Let's say the order did explicitly restrict moving out of state, but you move anyway. What happens? Because you're violating the current order, a judge would most likely hold you in contempt of court. The judge may also require you to pay the other parent's attorney's fees (in addition to your own).

More importantly, making a unilateral move could influence how the court views your judgment going forward. The court may tend to believe that you will make decisions impulsively or based only on what you want rather than planning and considering the children's best interests.

While you may not have technically violated the order if visitation is still possible, the judge may not approve of you suddenly moving to another state without first advising the court.

But who cares whether the judge ultimately approves of your move?

The problem is that judges don't like it when parents make drastic moves that affect the children without having an agreement or a hearing first. Most judges would not look kindly on one parent moving out of state without addressing custody beforehand. This kind of short-term action could have long-term consequences.

A judge may ultimately deny the children's move or, in a worst-case scenario, give custody to the other parent.

It is almost always better to file the motion for custody first and have it heard before you move. This shows your respect for the court process and for the other parent. Most importantly, it demonstrates your willingness to act in the best interests of the children.

What if you need to move quickly? Your best course of action is to explain the circumstances and request a hearing as soon as possible. Understandably, this can be a real hassle when you already have a million things to do to move. But these are the issues that you must deal with when you share custody of your children.

What If You Don't Have a Custody Order, but a Separation Agreement Addresses Custody?

Now let's suppose that you don't have a court order, but your separation agreement does detail the terms of custody. That agreement includes a clause that prohibits either parent from moving out of state without the other parent's written permission.

To modify the terms of a separation agreement, the other parent must agree to the modification. Otherwise, you'll have to file a new action for custody with the court.

So, let's assume again that your ex-husband will not agree to your move to Seattle with the kids. You file a case asking the court to decide custody.

In this scenario, if you move before the judge rules on the matter, you immediately violate the separation agreement.

What might happen if you move anyway? Most separation agreements include provisions for payment of the other parent's attorney's fees if the agreement is breached. And again, making such a drastic move without an agreement with the other parent or input from the court could influence how the court views your judgment.

The Home State

As a matter of terminology, a child's *home state* is the state where he or she has lived for the last 6 months. That means that state has jurisdiction over custody of the child. If you and the children leave the home state without adequately addressing custody issues, you are removing the child from his or her home state.

Why would this matter? In this situation, the other parent could easily file an **ex parte custody action** in court. This action alleges that the child has been removed from his or her home state without permission. The court could issue an order requiring you to return the child to the home state. The other parent could then take this court order to the local police department—in this case, in Seattle—and local law enforcement would assist in enforcing the order by retrieving the child to return to the other parent.

Ex parte custody actions are allowed so that parents cannot jump from state to state with their children. To avoid this problem, jurisdiction is proper in the state where the child has resided for the past six months. Otherwise, there would be no way to control the movement of children or determine which state could issue custody orders.

Could You Ever Move First with the Children and then File with the Court or File with the Court and Leave Simultaneously?

Maybe. Domestic violence could be a valid basis to move first and file later or to file simultaneously with a move. If the other parent's conduct has been consistently threatening and you truly fear for the safety of the children or yourself, then, in some circumstances, moving immediately may be not just possible, but preferable.

It may still be best to file an ex parte domestic violence protective order. This will alert the court about your intent to move temporarily and allow the court to quickly hear your case on emergency custody.

What if there's no violence, but you have a financial crisis? Financial issues are always a concern for parents. If you need to move because of unexpected and uncontrollable financial issues, you may feel that you need to move immediately and have a custody hearing later. This can be tricky, especially if the court believes that your financial issues were self-imposed. You could still face the other consequences we discussed above. It is best to talk to an attorney before you move, even for a financial emergency.

If the Other Party Has Only Minimal Visitation, Wouldn't It Be Okay for Me to Move First and Address Custody Later?

It may be easier to move if the other parent has only minimal visitation, but it doesn't mean that you can just pick up and go. You still need to either reach an agreement with the other parent or get the court's permission with a modified order. Sure, you could take the risk and move without modifying the arrangement. But in the long term, that will probably hurt your case. You could suffer the sanctions mentioned above, and you may also find yourself having to ask the court to forgive your actions.

Certainly, a unique situation may arise that calls for you to move quickly. You may decide that you have to move first and answer the court's questions later. Just know that this is rarely the best choice, even when the other party doesn't have extensive visitation rights.

So, What Should You Really Do First?

First, take a step back and calmly assess your reasons for the relocation. Is this move really in the best interests of your children? For just a moment, forget about what is best for you. Focus on what is best for the children and how the move will affect them.

Second, discuss your situation with your attorney. Every district and every judge will have a different approach to relocation. Your attorney will know how these types of cases are usually treated in your district. You may be at the mercy of the judge, but it is rarely to your advantage to move first and ask questions later.

When it comes to child custody and relocation, the aptly named North Carolina case *Frey v. Best* said it best:

Naturally, no hard and fast rule can be laid down for making this determination, but each case must be determined upon its own peculiar facts and circumstances.

Judges are human, and their own personal experiences and emotions will surely play into these cases. It is best to go into these matters with your eyes wide open, aware of the "peculiar facts and circumstances" of your own situation as well as the potential consequences of relocating without the court's permission.

WHO HAS JURISDICTION
IN CHILD CUSTODY MATTERS?

When parents file a custody lawsuit, their first allegations must relate to why and how the state where they filed the case has jurisdiction to hear the matter. When it comes to minor children, a state must have *jurisdiction* over the child or children in question. For a state to have jurisdiction over a child, it must be the state of the child's residency. For children, this state with residency is called the child's *home state*.

In North Carolina, "home state" means the state where a child lived with a parent or a person acting as a parent for at least six consecutive months before the start of the child custody proceeding. If the child is less than six months old, the home state is the state where the child has lived from birth with a parent or someone acting as a parent. Temporary absences from the state do not affect the six-month period.

How the "Home State" Rule Affects Custody

Let's look at a new example to see this in action. Allen and Cindy have lived in New York City for five years. Their two sons were both born in New York. Originally, both Allen and Cindy are from eastern North Carolina. Cindy never wanted to leave North Carolina. They only came to New York for Allen's job. Sadly, they have now decided to separate. Cindy wants to move back to North Carolina right away. Allen could see the children when he comes to visit his own family. Since both Allen and Cindy are from North Carolina, a North

Carolina court would decide child custody, right? Wrong.

Allen and Cindy may originally be from North Carolina, but their children aren't. Their children are citizens and residents of New York. Allen and Cindy are also citizens and residents of New York, even though they were born in North Carolina. They have lived in New York long enough for their residency to have changed.

Why Must Custody for Allen and Cindy's Children Be Decided in New York?

Remember that Allen and Cindy's children have lived in New York their entire lives. Therefore, New York, not North Carolina, is their "home state." A New York court will decide their custody case. That means that Cindy cannot file a child custody action in North Carolina. If she did, Allen could ask the court to dismiss the action because North Carolina lacks jurisdiction over the children.

This residency requirement exists to prevent parents from *"forum shopping."* Forum shopping refers to parents attempting to pick a state that they think may look more favorably on their custody matter. In Cindy's case, North Carolina courts are more convenient for her since she's moving there.

As with all matters of the law, there is a caveat. If the case involves domestic violence, Cindy may be able to go to court in North Carolina and gain a temporary custody order. However, the North Carolina court would still almost certainly require Cindy to return to New York to fully resolve custody.

Domestic violence requires a different approach in all situations related to custody matters. Different rules often apply, at least temporarily, to protect the abused parent. These rules are intended to keep everyone safe until the custody matter can be fully heard by the court that has jurisdiction.

What Would Happen If Cindy Moved with the Children and No Child Custody Action Were Filed in New York?

If Allen does not consent to Cindy moving back to North Carolina and taking the kids, he should file a custody action in New York to have the children returned there, where a New York court would resolve their custody.

What if it's clear that Cindy is trying to avoid the jurisdiction of the New York courts? Allen could most likely obtain an order requiring Cindy to return with the children to New York immediately or, in the alternative, to return the children to Allen until a custody hearing can be scheduled.

But wouldn't Cindy be kidnapping the children if she moved them to North Carolina without Allen's permission? In most cases, the situation would not rise to the level of kidnapping. The North Carolina criminal statute, like most state laws about kidnapping, is very specific on what constitutes this crime. The more likely remedy would be an emergency custody order.

Can North Carolina Relinquish or Transfer Jurisdiction to Another State After Deciding Custody?

North Carolina law establishes two circumstances where a court of another state could obtain jurisdiction after a North Carolina court issues a custody order. Another state could gain jurisdiction over the child when one of the following is true:

1. *A court of [North Carolina] determines that [ ] the child, the child's parents, and any other person acting as a parent do not have a significant connection with this State and that substantial evidence is no longer available in this State concerning the child's care,*

protection, training and personal relationships; or

2. *A court of this State or a court of another state determines that the child, the child's parents, and any person acting as a parent do not presently reside in this State.*

Confusing? Let's look at another example. Say that a North Carolina court awards a mother custody of a child and allows her to permanently move out of North Carolina and into another state. The judge may also transfer the order and jurisdiction in the case to the state of the child's new residence.

What if a North Carolina court enters a custody order but then both parents and their children move to another state? They could register the custody order in that state. This process grants the new state jurisdiction to hear and enforce any disputes concerning custody. Going forward, the new state could decide any new custody issues as if it had made the original custody determination.

What If Cindy Came Here From Another Country and Wanted to Move Back There?

If Cindy took the children to another country without Allen's permission, intending to avoid jurisdiction in the United States, she could be committing an international child abduction. That's a very serious offense.

What the Hague Convention Says

An international treaty called the Hague Convention on the Civil Aspects of International Child Abduction addresses these specific situations.

Generally speaking, the Hague Convention prevents one parent from wrongfully taking children under the age of 16 from their country of habitual residence and into another country that hasn't been their habitual residence. The goal of the treaty is to return children to their status quo that existed before the wrongful removal. The courts of the children's home country should decide the custody dispute.

The treaty doesn't define *habitual residence*. It basically means the country of the children's ordinary or customary residence before the wrongful removal.

Can Allen Recover His Children?

Let's return to our example with Allen and Cindy. Allen, the parent left behind in the United States without the children, would be called the *petitioner*, the person who files the case. Allen has the burden of proving that Cindy wrongfully removed the children. As the petitioner, Allen must show three things:

1. the children resided habitually or regularly in Allen's country, the United States, at the time of the removal,

2. the removal of the children violated Allen's custody rights under U.S. law, and

3. Allen was exercising those custody rights when Cindy removed the children.

The goals are to avoid having one parent disregard the custodial rights of the other parent and to prevent a parent from seeking refuge in another country that may have more sympathetic laws or courts. Under the Hague Convention, the court that hears the action does not consider the merits of the underlying custody dispute. Instead, it only determines what country should hear those issues. The custody dispute itself is then returned to the appropriate country.

Cindy, as the person who removed the children, is referred to as the **respondent.** In response to Allen's allegations that she wrongfully removed the children from their country of habitual residence, Cindy can assert four types of defenses under the Hague Convention. She can argue any of the following:

1. There is a major risk of harm to the children if they are returned, or the children would be placed in an intolerable situation if they are returned.

2. Return of the children would violate the fundamental principles of the United States relating to human rights and basic freedoms.

3. The petitioner did not file the action for the return of the children within one year of the wrongful removal, and now the children are settled in the new country.

4. The petitioner, Allen, was not exercising his rights of custody at the time of the removal.

If your child has been wrongfully removed from this country to another country, seek legal advice immediately. You must take action as quickly as possible to preserve your rights.

What Does This Mean for Your Custody Case?

Custody matters must be decided in a state that has jurisdiction. Parents cannot run around the country—or the globe—looking for courts that might be sympathetic to their desires for a custodial arrangement. Talk to an attorney and know your rights so that you can pursue your case in the appropriate forum.

RELOCATION
FOR BETTER JOB OPPORTUNITIES

Many people are on the lookout for a new or different job. The reasons vary, whether it's higher pay, increased recognition, or more predictable or flexible hours. Some people are ready to change careers completely or to start over in a new place.

Unsurprisingly, many of these people are parents. These job-seeking parents are often looking for ways to better the lives of their families, especially their children. But for those parents who share custody, how will moving affect their custody arrangements? Read on to find out.

A Review of How Custody Orders Are Modified

You'll remember that child custody can be decided by agreement or by the court. If parents reach an agreed custody arrangement, they may leave that as a private contract between themselves. If so, future changes are also up to the parents to resolve between themselves. In the alternative, parents who reach an agreement may ask the court to enter it as a consent custody order.

If the parents fail to agree on custody, the court can hear the case and reach its own decision about what is in the best interests of the children. In that case, the court will again memorialize its decision as an order.

Once a court order for custody is entered, regardless of whether it is reached by consent or by the court, the parents must file a motion to modify the order to change its terms. Again, such a modification can be made by agreement or decided by the court.

Remember that when the court makes the decision, it follows a two-part test:

1. Has a substantial change of circumstances affecting the welfare of the children occurred since the entry of the last order?

2. If a substantial change of circumstances has occurred, what is in the children's best interests given those new circumstances?

As with all child custody decisions, courts decide whether relocation for a new job warrants modification of an existing custody order on a case-by-case basis. Every situation is different, so your case will be judged based on its specific facts.

Benefits of a Job Change

Usually, a voluntary job change will be accompanied by improvements in the parent's quality or standard of living.

Some parents have jobs that require them to work second shift, so they're never at home in the evenings with their children. Some parents have to put in 60 or more hours a week to meet deadlines or earn enough money. Those long hours often mean they have less time at home with the children and miss the most basic of activities, such as family dinner or a bedtime story.

Some parents have jobs that require them to travel or endure a long commute; others have low-paying jobs and thus struggle to make ends meet each month.

Whatever the reason, for some parents, a new job can bring great benefits to their children and families. Less travel or fewer hours in the office can allow for extra time each day or week with the children. Higher pay makes it much easier to provide clothes, food, health care, school supplies, and other essentials for the children.

However, for parents who live apart from their co-parents, whether they were never married or have divorced, getting a new job could pose a problem.

When a Change in Jobs Demands Relocation

What if that great new job, the one with extra pay or fewer hours, also requires the parent to move several hours away or out of state? The extra pay or decreased hours certainly could benefit the children, but how does a proposed relocation affect custody?

Because these situations have so many possible permutations, let's look at three separate examples of parents who need their custody arrangements modified because of their new jobs.

A New Job With Fewer Hours

Our first couple, Adam and Andrea, had three school-aged children when they separated. Adam is a cardiologist at the hospital in Asheville, and Andrea is a local real estate agent. Throughout their marriage, Adam has always had an irregular work schedule that is largely out of his control, while Andrea has always had flexible hours.

Long and Unpredictable Hours at the Previous Job

At the hospital, Adam works 12-hour shifts four days a week, not counting the time he is on call. Sometimes those 12-hour days turn into 16-hour days. When he is on call, days off can turn into workdays. Some weeks Adam works during the day, while others he works nights. Every now and then, he has to work on a holiday.

Adam and Andrea have been separated and divorced for two years. Soon after their separation, they entered into a consent court order that laid out their custody terms.

Since Adam worked so many hours and had an unpredictable

schedule, he was not able to commit to much time with his three children. As the children are getting older, Adam is tired of missing out on their lives.

New Job Has Shorter, Predictable Hours

After a thorough job search, Adam has been offered a full-time position with East Carolina University's medical school as a professor and research director in cardiology. However, this position will require Adam to relocate from Asheville to Greenville, which is five hours away at the opposite end of the state.

The upside to Adam's new position is that he will now be working only during traditional business hours: no more 16-hour days, no more working through the night, and no more weekends stuck in the hospital. Perhaps best of all, he won't have to work on holidays.

This new position will provide Adam much more flexibility for spending time with his children. However, Adam is concerned about how the relocation will affect the custody order that he and Andrea have in place.

Adam and Andrea cannot agree on a solution, so Adam files a motion asking the court to modify the custody order.

Adam knows that to modify his custody order, there must be a substantial change of circumstances—something big enough that it affects the children's well-being. He also knows that he must show the judge that his relocation would benefit the children and that there is a direct link between the relocation and the benefit.

There is a Substantial Change in Circumstances

In this case, the judge determined that Adam's new job and subsequent relocation constitutes a substantial change of circumstances affecting the well-being of the three children.

Adam's home will now be far from Andrea's, but his work schedule will go from hectic and unpredictable to the exact opposite: reliable and predictable. This will allow Adam to spend significantly more time with the children.

The Change is Beneficial to the Children

Not only is the new job and relocation a substantial change of circumstances, but it also positively affects the well-being of Adam and Andrea's three children. In short, Adam's relocation for this new job would benefit all three children.

While working at the hospital, Adam frequently had to miss holidays, birthdays, parent-teacher conferences, baseball games, and even vacations with the children. His new job will allow him to plan for and partake in all of these events. Instead of the children spending a single day here or there with Adam, they will now be able to spend many consecutive days with him. This could mean visiting over various weekends, spending half of Christmas break with him, and enjoying several weeks together in the summer. Adam will now be able to spend time with the children on holidays and even take them on vacations in the summer.

This time will give the kids an opportunity to strengthen their critical relationship with their father.

The Court Modifies the Custody Order

Overall, the new job is a win for the kids. They will be able to gain significant quality time with Adam that they could never have while he was in his hospital job. Even though he will live farther away from their residence with Andrea, he will be able to plan for visits and devote more time to the children.

Adam has successfully shown the judge that his new job and relocation are a substantial change of circumstances that positively affects the well-being of the children. Therefore, the court agrees to modify the custody order.

A New Job with Higher Pay

John and Jackie have been separated and divorced for five years. They have two children, who are 13 and 11. John lives in Raleigh and works in the IT field; Jackie lives in Charlotte and works at her family's restaurant.

According to their custody order, the children reside with John when school is in session. They travel to Charlotte to stay with Jackie whenever school is out.

Since they've had the custody order in place, Jackie has canceled some of the children's visits with her. She has not stayed up to date with the children's academic progress or with their routine medical appointments and needs.

John is Laid Off

Last month, John found out he was being laid off by his company at the end of the month. This meant the income he has been comfortable with—the money that has helped support his two children—would end. He, like all of us, has bills to pay and mouths to feed.

John immediately started a job search. Within just three weeks, he received an offer for a different type of IT job. However, this new position would require him to relocate to the company's national headquarters in Florida.

Prospects for the New Job

Despite the relocation, the new job promised some great advantages.

John's salary would immediately increase by $20,000 annually. Health insurance benefits for himself and the children would be less expensive. The new job even promised regular promotions to managerial positions in the years to come—meaning more pay raises.

However, it would impossible for the children to see Jackie as often as they have. In North Carolina, John and Jackie only live about three hours apart. The distance from Florida would be too great to continue regular visits without putting a strain on the children.

Jackie doesn't want John to take the children with him to Florida. They are familiar with her home in Charlotte, and they get to see many of her family members, who live nearby.

John needs a job, and this one offers beneficial prospects for John and his career. He files a motion to modify the custody order.

There is a Substantial Change of Circumstances

A move to Florida, plus the potential advancement opportunities for John's career, would mean a substantial change of circumstances affecting the well-being of John and Jackie's children.

John's salary would significantly increase, he would have health insurance for the children, and he would have the possibility of career advancement.

All of these factors would affect the well-being of the children. John's ability to provide for his children financially would improve. The children would have access to private health insurance. As John's career advanced, he would be better able to keep up with increases in the costs of the children's educational and extracurricular activities.

The Change Benefits the Children

Overall, John and Jackie's children would benefit from John's new job, despite the relocation and missed visits.

John's higher salary would ensure that the children's needs were well provided for, including food, clothing, and school supplies. The kids would also benefit from affordable health-care options. Plus, as John's salary increased, the children would be able to participate in extracurricular activities that come at a cost to parents.

Although John and Jackie have always been able to provide for the children, John's increased earning potential provides extra assurance that the children will be well taken care of. Because Jackie hasn't taken full advantage of her custodial role, her arguments about the distance reducing her visitation are less effective. All told, John's new job seems to be a win-win situation for the children.

The Court Modifies the Custody Order

The judge finds that a substantial change in circumstances affecting the well-being of the children has occurred. He also finds that this change would benefit the children.

Again, Jackie has missed custodial periods with the children and has not kept herself informed about their general welfare. Therefore, moving with John would be in the best interests of the children.

John's new job with higher pay puts the children in a better position to flourish despite the decrease in visitation with Jackie. In total, it is appropriate to modify the custody order, and the court does.

A New Job with Different Hours

Harold and Hannah never married but had one child together, a little girl who is now nine years old. A consent custody order has been in place since their daughter was six months old.

The custody order gave Harold and Hannah equal custody. They have always operated under a 2-2-3 schedule: Hannah has their daughter on Mondays and Tuesdays, Harold has Wednesdays and Thursdays, and they alternate three-day weekends.

Harold, a pharmacist, has always worked traditional business hours at a small, independently owned pharmacy. Hannah, a nurse at a pediatrician's office, also keeps a reliable schedule with standard hours.

A Job Change is Needed

The economy has begun to affect the small pharmacy where Harold works. The owners have talked about closing it. So, Harold begins to look for a new job that would provide better long-term stability and advance his career path.

After months of searching, he decides to accept a job at a major national pharmacy chain.

The new job promises Harold increased pay and great benefits. Unfortunately, he will have to relocate to the next county, a little over an hour away. He will also have to work more irregular hours. His new schedule will have him working every other weekend and until 10:00 some nights.

Harold believes that he can arrange his new work schedule so that he is off on the days and nights that he has his daughter. He also plans to alternate his work weekends with her weekends.

However, if his daughter stays with Harold in his new location, she would then have an hour-long drive to and from school. Harold thinks this inconvenience would be offset by his ability to earn a greater salary with better benefits.

Hannah does not agree with putting their daughter on the road so much. She believes that the extra hour commuting would cut into their daughter's time for homework, extracurricular and social activities, and a good night's sleep.

This is Not a Substantial Change of Circumstances

In this situation, there is not a substantial change of circumstances affecting the well-being of Harold and Hannah's daughter.

First, note that the current custody arrangement can still be followed. While Harold will spend more time driving, he will not live so far away or work such long hours that he cannot keep his end of the agreement.

Second, while their daughter will be on the road more frequently, there is no evidence that this would negatively affect her. Hannah makes good points that the additional driving time would cut into the time available for schoolwork and extracurricular activities. Still, nothing suggests that this would be a disservice to her.

There are no indications that the child cannot continue to flourish academically or participate in her current extracurricular activities. Despite the increased and nontraditional work hours, Harold can arrange his schedule so it has little or no impact on his time with his daughter.

For these reasons, it would be inappropriate to modify Harold and Hannah's custody order.

What Happens If You Have to Relocate for a New Job?

It depends! Each situation is different. As with all family law matters, the court will determine whether to modify its custody order for your new job by considering the specific circumstances of your family. These decisions are always made on a case-by-case basis, as each family is unique.

As the above examples illustrate, two rules hold fast, regardless of the situation. First, the new job must create a substantial change in circumstances. And, of course, any modification based on the new job must serve the best interests of the children.

RELOCATION
FOR MARRIAGE OR REMARRIAGE

"I am getting married, moving across the country, and taking our child with me."

What do you do when your ex tells you this? Where do you even begin? Maybe you go into panic mode. Maybe you are angry. All that your son has ever known is in North Carolina. All of your family is here. Your daughter is excelling in school and in her extracurricular activities. You have never lived that far away from your children. They need you around. Maybe you don't even like your ex's new partner, and there's no way you want your kids living with that person. What if the new partner has a criminal history? Do you even know that he or she doesn't?

You may think there is no way any judge would ever agree to your ex moving so far away and taking your child. But what if the judge did agree? Is that possible?

Or maybe you are the one who is remarrying. You have finally found someone that you want to spend your life with. You know this is the person for you. Your kids love your partner, and he or she loves them. Finally, your life is going great, but you have a custody order in place that won't work in your new life. Your soon-to-be new spouse is in another state or a long way from where you and your children currently live. There is no way you can continue to follow your custody order. You will need to have it modified. Surely, your co-parent can see how well the kids are doing and how great a stepparent your new partner will be.

Will the judge allow you to modify your custody order? What if the judge denies your motion to modify the order? What will you do?

In this chapter, we'll talk about what happens when a parent is relocating for a new relationship and about the situations where a judge may grant or deny a request to modify a custody order.

(Re-)Marriage by Itself

Suppose your ex tells you that he or she is getting married (or remarried) but will continue to live locally. The problem is that you have never even met this new person—or you have, and you do not like him or her. You have no idea what kind of person he or she is. What kind of stepparent will he or she be? You do not want your children around this mystery person! And what if he or she already has children? What do you know about them? Nothing! So, you decide to have your custody order modified.

You do some research and discuss with your lawyer the reasons you want to modify your custody order. You already know that you must have a substantial change in circumstances affecting the children's well-being before the court will modify the order.

Is marriage or remarriage a substantial change in circumstances? Your children will be affected. They will gain a stepparent, and another adult will be living in the home with them. Is this enough to modify custody?

A New Relationship is Not Enough to Modify Custody

Unfortunately, marriage or remarriage alone, with no other factors, is not enough to count as a substantial change in circumstances affecting the children's well-being.

So what does it take to have a substantial change in circumstances, particularly when a parent's new relationship involves a relocation?

There Must Be Both a Disruption and a Direct Link

To meet the modification standard of a substantial change in circumstances affecting the children's well-being, you must be able to show two things:

1. that the marriage and the subsequent relocation would be disruptive to the children, and

2. that there is a direct link between the relocation and the disruption.

An Example with No Showing of Disruption

John and Julie have a daughter together named Jessica. John and Julie separated and eventually divorced when Jessica was two. All three have lived in the same county of North Carolina, both before and after the separation. During the separation period, they negotiated a custody arrangement that was entered as a consent court order for child custody. Under the order, Jessica lived with Julie during the week and with John on weekends. Holidays and summer vacations were divided evenly between Julie and John.

Julie Remarries and Plans to Relocate with the Child

A few years later, Julie met Bob and fell in love. They married when Jessica was eight. The problem is that Bob lives and works in New York. Before meeting Bob, neither Julie nor Jessica had ever been to New York. Julie has no family or friends in New York other than Bob.

Julie assumed that since she has primary physical custody of Jessica, they could easily move to New York to live with Bob. John could still see Jessica sometimes to maintain their father-daughter relationship. It might not be every weekend like it has been, but he would not be cut off completely from Jessica.

Julie talked with John about her plans to move to New York to be with her new husband and to take Jessica with her. She indicated that she would look for a job there, but she didn't have one yet. Similarly, she planned to enroll Jessica in school in New York.

But Jessica Is Only Familiar With North Carolina

John was understandably angry. He could not believe that Julie would even think about relocating and taking their daughter so far away. John had maintained his same residence in the same county since he and Julie separated. He had a good, stable job. Even all of Jessica's extended family lived in North Carolina, including her grandparents, aunts, uncles, and cousins. Jessica has lived in the same area for all eight years of her life. This is all that she is familiar with—it's what she knows. John thought surely a judge would modify the custody order to grant him primary physical custody instead.

So, John filed a motion to modify their consent court order. He argued that a substantial change of circumstances affecting Jessica's well-being had occurred: namely, Julie had remarried and planned to relocate with Jessica to another state.

John Argues that the Relocation
Would Put the Child in Strange Surroundings

The judge held a hearing on John's motion. Both parents presented evidence and testified. Since it was John's motion, he had the burden of showing the judge that a substantial change in circumstances affecting Jessica's well-being had occurred.

In the hearing, John argued that Julie's proposed move to New York with Jessica would disrupt his visitation schedule. He needed those visits to maintain the strong father-daughter relationship he had with Jessica and to ensure that she had enough quality time with her dad. Further, John argued that Jessica would be living in a new house in a new city with a new stepparent and attending a new school with new classmates.

This whole move would be strange and unfamiliar to Jessica.

The Judge's Ruling: No Disruption, No Direct Link

To John's surprise, the judge denied his motion to modify the child custody order. The judge stated that John did not adequately show that Julie's proposed move to New York after a remarriage would disrupt Jessica's well-being. The only evidence that John presented in the hearing was about how his relationship with Jessica would be affected and how the move would put Jessica in unfamiliar surroundings.

Note that courts do not automatically assume that changes—even major changes like the ones that Jessica would experience with a move to New York—are disruptive or negative experiences for a child.

The judge needed John to demonstrate a direct link between the remarriage, the relocation, and his daughter's well-being. Because John did not show that direct link, the judge could not determine that there was a substantial change in circumstances affecting Jessica's well-being due to the relocation.

An Example of a Clear Showing of Disruption

Let's change some facts in the scenario of John, Julie, and Jessica. Julie has still married Bob and is proposing that she and Jessica move to New York to live with Bob. But now, suppose that John presented more detailed facts at the hearing on his motion to modify the custody order.

Jessica Has an Excellent Relationship with Both Parents

At the hearing, John presented evidence directly addressing Jessica's well-being. Jessica has a very close relationship with both of her parents and gets along with them equally. She sees each parent regularly and enjoys spending time with each parent. Jessica frequently participates in extended family functions with both her mother's family and her father's family, who all live locally.

Jessica Has Strong Extracurricular Connections and Friendships

Furthermore, John provided evidence that Jessica is excelling in her school in North Carolina. Both John and Julie are involved with her progress in school, and both maintain contact with her teachers. Jessica regularly participates in extracurricular activities and has established strong friendships with children her age. Jessica has developed and maintained strong connections in both parents' neighborhoods.

In short, both parents are highly involved in Jessica's mental, physical, and educational development and well-being.

Jessica Has Begun to Express Fears of Relocating

John testified that he and Julie have gotten along fairly well in the past and have been able to co-parent in a positive way to Jessica's benefit. But ever since Julie remarried and told John that she was moving out of state to live with her new husband, their dynamic has deteriorated. John and Julie have argued about what is in Jessica's best interest and how Julie's remarriage and relocation would affect her well-being.

Eight-year-old Jessica has noticed the tension between her parents. Jessica has started asking questions about what would happen with John if she moved to New York. She has expressed fears of not being able to see both parents, her extended family on both sides, and her friends from school and extracurricular activities.

Jessica Has Exhibited Anxiety About Relocating

Recently, at a custody exchange, Jessica even exhibited what John called separation anxiety. Jessica started crying and seemed fearful of leaving John to go with Julie. Jessica said she was not sure when she was moving to New York and feared it would happen right away.

The Judge's Ruling: Disruption Shown with a Direct Link

With these additional facts, the judge granted John's motion to modify the child custody order. The judge found a substantial change in circumstances affecting Jessica's well-being. He ruled that a move to New York would disrupt Jessica. Further, the judge drew a direct link between Julie's remarriage with its accompanying relocation and Jessica's well-being.

This time, the remarriage and proposed relocation had already begun to negatively affect Jessica. She had directly expressed her fears about Julie moving out of state to be with Bob. The judge agreed with John that a move to New York would disrupt Jessica's stable and frequent contact with John and all of her extended family on both sides. Further, the move would disrupt the friendships and extracurricular activities that Jessica has established.

The Relocation Does Not Benefit Jessica

The judge was unable to determine that a move to New York to live with Julie and her new husband would offer Jessica any advantages educationally, socially, or culturally compared to what she already had in North Carolina. The judge even hinted that Julie's proposed move out of state to live with her new husband was not to benefit Jessica but to satisfy her own selfish needs.

Another Example of a Showing of Disruption

Kyle and Karen have a 13-year-old daughter, Kelly. Kyle and Karen have been divorced for several years. Their established joint custody order has worked well and to Kelly's benefit over the years.

But then Karen meets Jack.

Karen Plans to Marry a Sex Offender

Karen and Jack become engaged. After they marry, Karen plans to move into Jack's house. Kyle has never met Jack. However, he finds out from one of Karen's friends that Jack was convicted in Virginia five years ago for a sex offense involving a 14-year-old girl. He digs a little deeper and finds out that at the time of Jack's offense, he was a teacher at a public school where he coached the girls' soccer team.

Kyle is shocked that Karen has never mentioned any of this to him.

Kyle immediately files a motion to modify custody because Karen's remarriage to a sex offender would adversely affect Kelly.

At the hearing on Kyle's motion, he presents evidence to the judge that Jack's victim from the charged offense five years ago was not his only victim. Further, Jack has not participated in treatment or shown any rehabilitation. Due to Karen's work schedule, Kelly would be alone after school with Jack for several hours. Kelly is the same age as Jack's previous victims.

The Judge's Ruling: Disruption Shown with a Direct Link

The judge grants Kyle's motion to modify the custody order. The judge rules that Karen's remarriage to Jack and her subsequent relocation to Jack's house would be disruptive to Kelly and would adversely affect her well-being. He finds a direct link between the remarriage, relocation, and Kelly's well-being. Such a remarriage and relocation would endanger Kelly. Note that this relocation does not involve a move out of the community; the disruption is due to the potentially dangerous situation created by allowing Kelly to live with a sexual predator.

The Bottom Line

For a parent's remarriage and subsequent relocation to create a substantial change in circumstances that would adversely affect your child's well-being, you must show evidence of a disruption in the child's life. You must also prove that a direct link exists between the relocation for the new relationship and the disruption.

A Strange and Unfamiliar Environment is Not Necessarily a Negative Disruption

Not being able to spend as much time with your child if the other parent remarries and moves away does not constitute a substantial change in circumstances affecting the well-being of your child. Likewise, the fact that your child will be in a strange and unfamiliar environment does not necessarily mean that there will be a negative effect on your child's well-being. In these cases, there is no direct link yet showing that the remarriage and move would cause a negative disruption for the child.

Showing a Disruption That Does Not Benefit Your Child is Enough to Prevent a Relocation

You may be able to establish a direct link by demonstrating specific facts to the court. Maybe you can show that a remarriage and relocation would pull your child away from well-established familial relationships, friendships, and activities. If these lost connections could cause your child to decline rather than flourish educationally, socially, and culturally, you may convince a court that there is a link between the relocation and a negative disruption.

Similarly, if a remarriage and relocation would put your child in harm's way, those facts can establish a direct link between the remarriage, relocation, and resulting disruption to your child.

Marriage and Relocation Must Benefit Your Child

Regardless of whether you or your ex is the one marrying and relocating, the new relationship and relocation must be to your child's benefit. You must be able to articulate reasons and provide evidence about the advantages for your child. Moreover, you must show that the relocation would not negatively affect your child's educational, social, or cultural well-being.

RELOCATION AND DOMESTIC VIOLENCE:
MOVING FAR AWAY FOR SAFETY

So far, we've discussed parents relocating and taking their children with them because of new and (mostly) positive changes. Perhaps they've been offered an exciting new job, they've remarried and started a new relationship, or they want to be closer to beloved family members. But sometimes parents feel they must leave their current surroundings to be safe from domestic violence.

Whether it's an ex-spouse, a new spouse, or a live-in significant other, domestic violence can be a serious and scary issue, especially when children are involved.

All too often, the only way that victims can protect themselves and their children is to relocate. In some cases, that might mean relocating far away from the abuser. But this can be easier said than done when a child custody schedule is in place.

In this chapter, we'll consider two examples of domestic violence where there is a substantial change in circumstances allowing a custody schedule to be modified.

But first, let's make sure we're all on the same page.

What is Domestic Violence?

Two legal requirements define domestic violence under North Carolina law. First, an aggressor must commit a specific violent act against a victim. Second, the aggressor must have a personal relationship with the victim.

Acts of Domestic Violence

North Carolina law specifies what acts constitute domestic violence. These acts are broader than the generic example of a husband beating up his wife.

Acts of domestic violence must involve one or more of the following:

- attempting to cause bodily injury,

- intentionally causing bodily injury,

- placing the victim or a member of the victim's family or household in fear of imminent serious bodily injury,

- causing the victim or a member of the victim's family or household to fear continued harassment,

- causing substantial emotional distress, or

- committing an illegal sex offense.

Actions that a victim takes in self-defense do not qualify as acts of domestic violence.

Within a Personal Relationship

There must be or have been a personal relationship between the person committing the act or acts of domestic violence and the victim. Domestic violence also includes the above acts if they are inflicted on a minor child in the victim's custody.

Two people have a qualifying *personal relationship* if they meet any of the following criteria:

- they are or were married,

- they have a child or children together,

- they're child and parent or someone acting as a parent,

- they live together or have lived together in the same household, or

- they are or have been dating, so long as they are of opposite sexes.

If an aggressor commits an act of domestic violence against a victim with whom he or she has a qualifying personal relationship, the victim is entitled to a domestic violence protective order against the aggressor.

A domestic violence order can address issues of custody as they relate to the acts of domestic violence, but a standard custody order supersedes any custodial terms in a domestic violence protective order.

An Example of Domestic Violence Involving Bodily Injury

Carl and Cathy met online. When they met, Carl lived in North Carolina, and Cathy lived in New Jersey. Their relationship evolved, and eventually Cathy left her hometown and her family and moved to North Carolina to be with Carl.

The two never married, but they had three children together. Once they broke up, Cathy filed an action asking the court to resolve custody. They now have a child custody court order in place dictating that they share custody. Carl and Cathy live about 45 minutes away from each other.

Because they have three children together, Carl and Cathy have to communicate quite often. Carl has always had an aggressive personality; however, his attitude and demeanor have changed for the worse over the years. Now, he is often mean and quick-tempered. It wouldn't surprise Cathy if one day he became violent.

Carl recently had back surgery and now he frequently has to take pain pills. These medications tend to worsen Carl's mood and violent tendencies.

Bodily Injury That is Intentionally Caused

Lately, Cathy has become concerned for her own safety and that of her children. Carl seems to be a loose cannon; any perceived slight can cause him to be angry.

One night, during an exchange of the children, Carl became very angry with Cathy. He pushed her against the wall, bruising her. All three children were in the room and saw it happen.

During their exchange the following week, Carl pushed Cathy down to the floor and dragged her around the room by her hair. Again, the children witnessed what happened.

By this point, Cathy was terrified of Carl. Her earlier fears had come true.

Cathy knows that the only way to protect herself, and most importantly her children, is to relocate far away from Carl. He knows exactly where Cathy lives, where she works, where the children attend school, and where they go for daycare and after-school care.

Cathy's safest, best option is to return to New Jersey with the children. However, the custody order gives Carl significant visitation.

Substantial Change in Circumstances

First, Cathy files a motion with the court asking for a domestic violence protective order, which the court grants.

Cathy then files a motion to modify the existing child custody order. She asks the court for permission to relocate back to New Jersey with all three children, cutting off their visits with Carl.

Note that the court considered two facts to find that domestic violence had occurred. First, Carl committed a qualifying act by intentionally causing bodily injury: he pushed Cathy against a wall and bruised her. Because they previously lived together and have children together, Carl and Cathy are in a personal relationship. The judge therefore determines that Carl has committed acts of domestic violence against Cathy.

The court also found that a substantial change in circumstances affecting the well-being of the children had occurred.

Since Carl committed acts of domestic violence in the presence of the children, significant custodial time with Carl could be dangerous for the children. Plus, Carl's frequent use of pain pills could impair his ability to adequately care for them.

Cathy has family and friends in New Jersey, which will give her a strong support system to help care for the children. She even has a full-time job already lined up, so she will be financially stable.

The judge allows Cathy to move to New Jersey with the children, agreeing that the relocation would benefit the children. They would be well cared for and safe. The move would allow the children to flourish without witnessing recurring violence. The judge permits Carl to have some visitation periods and creates a new custodial schedule taking the long distance into account.

But what if there hasn't yet been this kind of obvious physical injury?

An Example of Domestic Violence Involving Substantial Emotional Distress

Tom and Toni were married for 10 years and had two children. When irreconcilable marital difficulties arose, they separated. Soon after, they entered into a child custody court order by consent.

The order granted Toni primary physical custody and Tom secondary physical custody. So, the children lived with Toni during the week for school and with Tom for a significant part of their time off from school, including weekends, holidays, and the summer. Tom and Toni live less than 15 minutes apart, but due to their work schedules, this was the best custodial schedule for their children.

They have now been divorced for five years. Over that time, Toni's personality has gradually changed. Now Tom sincerely believes that Toni may be mentally unstable.

Substantial Emotional Distress

These days, Toni continually tries to undermine Tom's parenting. If Tom disciplines the children by grounding them or taking away a prized item, Toni immediately revokes the punishment or returns the item, even buying a new one if necessary.

Toni badmouths Tom on Facebook and publicly criticizes his parenting. She even tells the kids what a bad person and father Tom is. Plus, she curses in front of the kids and while talking about Tom.

Recently, Tom planned a cruise for the kids. He notified Toni of this trip according to the vacation provisions of their custody order. Instead of agreeing, Toni bought her own last-minute cruise with the kids. Upon their return, she told Tom that the children did not want to go on another cruise because they already went on one with her.

More and more frequently, Tom misses his scheduled custodial periods with the kids because Toni refuses to allow the children to go to his house. She doesn't meet Tom when she's supposed to. Additionally, she and the kids are not at home during the scheduled exchange times, which prevents Tom from seeing the children.

Tom hardly sees his kids anymore. When he does, Toni berates him with derogatory remarks about his parenting ability.

Plausible Threats of Physical Injury

While Toni has not yet acted on her threats, she has repeatedly threatened to come to Tom's house and physically injure him if he tries to see the kids on certain occasions. Tom is afraid that Toni is being serious and is capable of following through with those threats.

Several times, Toni's threats have prevented Tom from coming to the kids' soccer games or school performances. Tom doesn't want to do anything that may cause Toni to harm or embarrass the kids.

Overall, Toni's actions are taking a major emotional toll on Tom and the children. She has disrupted the relationship and bond that Tom has with his children.

Tom believes the safest and best thing to do is to relocate, with the children, away from Toni. He files a motion to modify the consent custody order. He tells the court that he wants to relocate to a residence about two hours away from Toni. This will enable him to get himself and the children away from Toni's mental instability. It will also protect all of them while still allowing the children to maintain some relationship with Toni.

Substantial Change in Circumstances

Again, Toni's behavior meets the criteria for domestic violence because it satisfies both required factors. First, Toni committed a qualifying act by causing Tom substantial emotional distress. This is not a one-time argument; it is a pattern of conduct that has affected Tom's ability to see his children. Second, because they were married and have children together, Toni and Tom are in a qualifying personal relationship.

The judge determines that a substantial change in circumstances affecting the well-being of the children has occurred.

Toni's actions show such extreme hostility toward Tom that it has detrimentally affected the kids. The children have missed out on significant amounts of time with their father and have had to endure Toni's bitter rants about him. The parent-child relationships between Tom and his children have suffered due to Toni's direct actions. Her threats have impeded Tom from spending time with the children.

Plus, Toni's continual undermining of Tom has negatively affected the children. They feel confused and upset when she degrades and disparages Tom in front of them. She also does not consider Tom's opinions about the best interests of the children. Nor does she allow him to participate in decision-making.

Tom's relocation with the kids would be beneficial to all of them. Tom has the ability to positively and safely promote a relationship between the children and Toni. Moreover, they would not be routinely subjected to their mother's hostility.

Perhaps most importantly, distance would help Tom to keep himself and the children safe in the event that Toni decided to act on her threats.

The judge allows Tom to relocate with the children. It modifies the custody schedule to give Tom primary physical custody and Toni secondary physical custody.

Domestic Violence and Separation Agreements

Now consider these same examples with a small change. Imagine that both couples had been married and had reached separation agreements that the court had not entered as custody orders.

Their separation agreements would have detailed these custodial arrangements, along with the property settlement, alimony settlement, and any child support payments.

In a separation agreement, the custody schedule is a legal contract between the parents. Parents who wish to relocate can't simply file a motion to modify custody because the court was never involved in the initial custody determination and did not formalize the agreement as a consent order.

If, several years after executing their separation agreements, Cathy and Tom experienced these same domestic violence issues, they would have to file a new custody action in court rather than a motion to modify.

Once in court, their cases would proceed much as they did under the consent order. The judge would hear the evidence about the domestic violence and the current custody agreements. The judge would then arrange custody based on the circumstances, determining whether a relocation is in the children's best interests.

RELOCATION
TO BE CLOSER TO FAMILY

Let's take a look at the story of Sally and Sam. Sam is career military. The family moved to Camp Lejeune in North Carolina 10 years ago. Sally has stayed in North Carolina because Sam has been deployed so many times that the military hasn't required her to move. Both Sally and Sam are originally from Arkansas. They have two children, ages seven and nine.

Sadly, the time apart during deployments has been too much. Sally and Sam are now getting a divorce. They don't hate each other; they just grew apart. Sally has never liked North Carolina, and she wants to move back to Arkansas with the children.

Unfortunately, Sam has to stay in North Carolina for 10 more years to complete his service and obtain full retirement benefits. He's never helped much with the children or the household because he is always gone.

Sally thinks it would be so nice to be close to extended family in Arkansas and finally have some help. Will a judge let her move home?

Let's examine a few scenarios. In all of these, we're assuming that Sam objects to the move, thus requiring a court hearing.

Neither Parent Has Family in the Current State

Neither Sally nor Sam has family in North Carolina. All of their family members live in Arkansas. Their children know both of their extended families and have seen both sides of the family regularly. Both sides of the family have visited North Carolina several times, and the children have spent time in Arkansas on numerous occasions.

Sam will continue to be deployed for several months at a time for at least three more years. That Sam will be away for months at a time may make a difference, and a judge may allow Sally to move back to Arkansas to be close to her family.

However, if the children are actively involved in their school and community and appear to be happy and well-adjusted in North Carolina, a judge might determine that uprooting the children is not what is best for them.

Let's change the scenario. Suppose Sam has been promoted. He will no longer be deployed and will work normal hours. He can be around in a way he has never been before and wants to help with the children daily. This could very well make a difference, and the judge may require the children to stay in North Carolina. The relationship with a parent will always be superior to relationships with other family members.

A Few Family Members Are in the Current State

Here's another scenario. After Sally had lived in North Carolina for about five years, Sam's dad passed away. Sam's mom, now living alone, decided that she would move to the same North Carolina city that Sally lives in. For the past few years, she has helped Sally tremendously with caring for the children. Sam's sister decided that she too wanted to live near Sally's family and her mother, so she moved to the same city as well. Sally really likes her a lot, and she is very helpful with the children.

Still, they are not Sally's family; they are Sam's. She loves them, but it is not the same as being with her family. Let's say again that Sam will still be deployed for several months at a time for at least a few more years. Sally would like to move home to be closer to her family. The children know her family and have seen them quite frequently despite the distance.

The problem here is that the kids have established a life in North Carolina that includes close relationships with members of Sam's family. The court may treat this scenario differently because the children have family connections in North Carolina.

In these scenarios, the paramount question involves what benefits the move provides for the children, not for the parent. What will the children be moving to? What are they leaving behind?

A Recent North Carolina Case Involving a Move for Family

Recently, a North Carolina court addressed the issue of relocating to be closer to family members. In this case, both parents lived in North Carolina, but their remaining family members all lived in New York.

A lawsuit for custody was pending before the court in North Carolina. The dad spent minimal time with the child. His visits were supervised due to his ongoing prescription drug problem. The dad also did not pay regular child support.

The child's mother lost her job and needed her family's assistance. She informed the father that she was moving back to New York with their child. They discussed the issue for a few weeks, during which the dad didn't seem to object to the move. However, on the eve of her move to New York, the dad said he did not want the mother and their child to move.

Despite his objection, the mom moved with the child to New York. The father then filed for a court hearing to resolve child custody.

A few months later, the court held a hearing on the matter. The judge awarded the mother custody of the child and allowed them to remain in New York. The court found that the mom had no nefarious intent when she moved. Moreover, the father was not paying regular child support, and the mom needed her family's financial and emotional assistance. Further, the dad had spent minimal time with the child even before the move to New York.

Still, the dad didn't come away empty-handed. The judge awarded him visitation once a month, but only if he paid the transportation costs for those visits.

Now, let's change the facts a little. Suppose the dad didn't have a drug problem, spent significant time with the child, and paid child support regularly. Even so, the mom decided to move without the court's or dad's permission. As you can imagine, the outcome may very well be different from the case above.

What Tends to Be the Deciding Factor in These Cases?

What actually tips the scale in your favor? It is hard to pinpoint, as all judges have preconceived notions about how to rule in these cases. Your attorney should be familiar with the judges in your jurisdiction, which can guide you as to how your particular facts may play out in court.

Over the past several years, more and more judges have been elected or appointed and assigned to the family law courtroom despite having no background or experience in family law. This makes the process increasingly difficult on clients and attorneys. Navigating the court system with unpredictable judges who have never been involved in family law cases is stressful, to say the least.

The key point to remember in relocation matters is that each case is fact specific, so the outcomes will hinge on the facts of each case. Every family is so unique in its needs that it is impossible to formulate a clear rule to apply in relocation cases.

As with most legal matters, you need the facts on your side, and you need to prove those facts in court. Of course, there may be facts in favor of both sides, so judges have to make tough decisions. Though many new judges lack family law experience, the hope is that they will assess the facts and decide in the best interests of the children.

RELOCATION
FOR BETTER EDUCATIONAL OPPORTUNITIES

Let's say that you have always wanted to be a veterinarian. Finally, you were accepted to a veterinary school in Texas. You live in North Carolina. You applied to N.C. State, but you didn't get in.

You have a little boy who is six years old. You share custody of him with your ex-husband. The two of you have a child custody order that outlines a week-on/week-off schedule.

The current custody arrangement will be impossible if you move to Texas for school. But this is your dream. And you can't leave your son behind. Won't a judge see that making this move with your son is the best thing for everyone involved? Your ex has a good income. He can afford to visit regularly. You can also contribute to travel expenses. Of course the court will allow you to move with your son, right?

In most cases, furthering your education is a terrific goal. However, when children are involved, moving for a parent's education complicates matters. There is a tough balance to strike between improving the family's overall long-term financial position and suffering the immediate effects on the parent-child relationship.

As we have discussed in every chapter, there are many factors to consider when a parent wants or needs to move.

In the long run, a move to further one parent's education usually benefits the entire family, since more education typically means higher income. But on the front end, it can be hard to see how the move would benefit the children, since they would be displaced from their current life.

The goal is to show the court how the move will benefit the children.

Let's Take a Step Back

Consider the following questions:

1. Is the move permanent or simply for the period you'll be attending school? How long will school take?

2. How much will your education affect the children? For example, how will you arrange for child care when you are in school?

3. Did you consider and/or apply to schools close to your current location?

4. What type of travel arrangements will you need to facilitate visitation?

5. After your education is complete, will you move back to where you live now, stay where you got your education, or apply to jobs in other cities?

6. Will the education truly provide long-term benefits, or is this simply an impulse decision because you need a change?

7. What is the financial impact of not furthering your education? What would happen if you maintained your current employment or income instead?

If you determine the move is necessary to further your station in life, then you need to start crafting your reasons and lining up your proof about how the move will benefit your child. Consider the schools, extracurricular activities, and so forth for your new location. How do those opportunities compare with your child's current life?

Again, a big deciding factor may well be the current custodial arrangement. The less time the other parent spends with the children, the more the odds favor your move. If the other parent spends significant time with the children now, it usually makes the decision more difficult. Judges do not like to reduce contact with an involved parent who will be left behind in the current state.

When going to school requires you to move far away from the other parent, you will want to consider all of your options. Of all of the reasons to move a child away from the other parent, this is most likely the least persuasive one. Why, you ask? Because, on its face, the move will always appear to be for your benefit, not the child's. So, you will need to truly assess how you can build and present a case to show how the move will benefit your child as well.

You'll need to carefully review the particular facts surrounding your educational opportunity with your attorney so that together you can determine your best course of action.

MOVING WITHOUT THE CHILDREN:
WHEN IT'S THAT IMPORTANT

Moving to another state without your children before your custody arrangement is modified or established isn't advisable. But we're looking at the worst-case scenarios here. Life happens. Sometimes an elderly parent needs you. You may be the only option.

Let's say your mom's neighbor just called. He had to take her to the hospital again—this time, she fell in the bathtub. You live in North Carolina, but your mom lives in Texas. She moved there years ago when her second husband took a job there. Even after he passed away, she never moved back to North Carolina.

You, an only child, are horrified by the news. You talk to the doctors at the hospital and learn that your mom can't continue living alone. She needs around-the-clock care. But there is no way you can put your mom in an assisted living home. She needs you to take care of her and be there for her. There is no one else to help.

But what about your two children? You know your ex would never allow you to take the children to Texas. You have to leave tonight.

Or, what if the out-of-state job offer you received requires you to move almost immediately? The increase in salary is so significant that turning the job down would be the worst financial move of your career. With this new job, your children would have everything they need and, for once, more! What do you do when you have to decide right away?

As we discussed in a previous chapter, you could move with the children and face the consequences later. But in this chapter, we'll explore the option of moving without the children and resolving custody after you've completed your move.

Can You Move Without the Kids?

Many times, life events happen so quickly that it's impossible to schedule and complete a court hearing before you have to move.

Your first option, in most situations, will be to talk with your co-parent. Will he or she agree to a move, at least temporarily? Remember that if you have a court order, you may still be violating the order, even if the other parent agrees to what you're doing.

If the other parent will not agree to the move, or if your move will violate a court order, the best approach is to have your lawyer quickly draft a motion or file a lawsuit to modify or establish custody. This motion or lawsuit should outline the reasons you need to move quickly and temporarily leave the children behind. If you have not had a discussion with the other parent, your lawyer may also want to send a letter directly to him or her. That letter can explain the situation and clarify your intentions. Usually, you'd send this letter simultaneously with the court filing so the other parent is on notice.

What to Do After You Move

You will want to begin the evidence-gathering process at your new location as soon as you arrive.

Upon arrival at your new location, take the following steps:

1. Prepare a space for each of your children at your new residence. Take pictures of the residence and every room in the residence. These will help you show the court that you are ready for your children to live with you.

2. Investigate the school district and identify the schooling options best suited for each of your children. Be prepared to present evidence regarding these options to the court. If you aren't sure

what to do, talk with your lawyer about the types of information that you could gather.

3. Depending on your children's ages, determine the types of extracurricular and social activities in the area that would benefit each of your children.

4. Brainstorm ways that the new location could benefit each of your children. For example, let's say you have a child with bad allergies. Perhaps the new location is home to one of the top allergy clinics in the region. Or maybe your child has a learning disability, and your new town offers free after-school tutoring to learning-disabled children. Gather information that you can bring to the court to explain these benefits.

5. If you would need child care, consider the type of care you would use and outline a care plan. Gather information about those services for the court.

6. Determine the travel options your children could use to return for visitation with the other parent. What is the closest airport? Could they take a train? Outline these options and their costs.

7. Tell your lawyer which extended family members are near your new home. Can they assist with child care and participate in your children's lives? Be ready to explain what these family members can do and how their presence will benefit your children.

8. Discuss with your lawyer any additional evidence that you can gather to show how the move will benefit your children.

What If I Move Without the Children and No Order Is in Place?

If no formal agreement or order is in place for custody and you need to move right away, file for custody with the court as soon as possible. Ideally, you'll be able to file simultaneously with your move or within just a few days thereafter. There is no real legal consequence at this point, except that you might be creating a status quo where the children live primarily with the other parent because you are absent.

Bear in mind that while you are away, the other parent has the opportunity to work on creating a stable life. Sometimes that will convince a judge to leave the children in their current situation, with the other parent. That's especially true if your new location doesn't offer any benefits that are far superior to what the kids already have.

The amount of time that the children spent with each parent before your departure is certainly important to the court. If, before the move, you were the primary caregiver, and you only left so abruptly because the situation mandated it, the court should consider those circumstances in making its decision.

Remember that we are talking here about emergencies. Moving without the children in the scenarios described above is very different from moving far away on a whim. We are not looking at flights of fancy such as moving for a new boyfriend or girlfriend or moving for a temporary and unimportant job opportunity. The urgent situations we outlined are legitimate reasons to move first and figure out a plan later.

What If an Order or Agreement is in Place?

Depending on the type of order or agreement you have, you could technically violate it by moving without the children. This could occur if your arrangement calls for you to spend significant time with the children and you are unable to do so after the move. However, it would be rare for the other parent to pursue that violation if he or she actually kept the kids during your absence.

If you move alone without the children, give adequate notice to the other parent about the situation and its urgency, and promptly file with the court to address custody, the court is unlikely to find that you violated the agreement or order.

Of course, if the other parent has minimal visitation and minimal ability to care for the children full-time, it may be best to take the children with you when you move. You would still need to file a motion explaining your situation as quickly as possible. While you may have to pay a premium to have a lawyer draft and file that expedited motion, it is worth the expense if it casts you in the best possible light to the court.

The more difficult scenario is when the children have significant time with both parents and you need to move immediately to another state. These are tough situations. Often, there is no good answer. You may face the luck of the draw as far as how your assigned judge views your case and whether that judge thinks you made the right decision. As upsetting as that may sound, unfortunately, it is often the harsh reality of custody matters.

What's the Bottom Line?

It can't be overstated that there are no easy answers in these challenging situations. Judges do understand that life happens. But sometimes judges have to make tough choices when one parent has to move far away. Yes, sometimes judges decide cases on their instincts. Sometimes there really is no rhyme or reason to why the judge picked one parent to have custody. Judges have to make a decision, just like you did, and it's not always the right decision.

If you are the parent who has significantly more time with the children, it may be easier for you to move and take the children. If both parents share significant time with the kids, the decision is usually much harder for the court. It would be nice if there were a magical formula or a crystal ball to see the future, but there isn't. Consult with a lawyer to plan your best course of action.

HOW CAN I OBTAIN
EVIDENCE IN ANOTHER STATE TO PRESENT IN COURT?

You live in North Carolina, as you have for several years. Now, though, you want to move to Florida for a great job opportunity. The neighborhood where you would live is full of children, and the schools are fantastic. There are countless extracurricular activities that your kids could participate in. Not to mention, you have numerous relatives who live near your new neighborhood.

You've filed a motion with the court proposing that you modify your custody order to move to Florida with the children. The court has set a hearing date. Now, how do you show the North Carolina court all the great benefits of Florida life for your children?

Witnesses and documents are the most common types of evidence that parties present at child custody hearings. The process is much easier when all the important witnesses and documents are in the state where the trial will actually take place. But that's generally not possible for cases involving long-distance relocations.

When witnesses and documents are not in the same state as the court that will hear your case, it can add a layer of complexity and expense to your child custody hearing.

How Can Witnesses from Another State Testify If They Can't Attend Your Hearing?

It's common for witnesses who live out of state to be unable to attend trial. Attending a trial may be cost prohibitive for out-of-state witnesses due to the expenses of travel or missed work. Witnesses also may not want to travel to court and testify for a variety of reasons.

What can you do?

One option is to arrange a *video deposition*. A deposition is recorded testimony that takes place outside of court, usually at an attorney's office. Parties can record depositions in one of two ways:

1. a court reporter or stenographer transcribes the witness's testimony, or

2. a video camera records the witness while testifying.

The more common method is for a court reporter or a stenographer to record testimony. However, where the witness is out of state and will not be present at trial, a video deposition allows the judge to actually see the person instead of just reading his or her answers.

If it is your witness being deposed, you would send legal notice to the other party of the deposition so that the other party and his or her attorney could be present, and vice versa.

As mentioned above, depositions typically take place at an attorney's office. During a deposition, the witness has to answer a lawyer's questions under oath, just as if he or she were in court. Where possible, both attorneys will question the witness on the same day to save everyone time and money.

Deposing a witness in another state is more costly. You also must follow different procedures if the witness will not submit voluntarily to the deposition. Compelling a witness to participate in a deposition will increase your costs as well.

Video depositions provide certain advantages but also come with their own disadvantages.

The Advantages of Video Depositions

Consider the following advantages of a video deposition:

1. If the witness is your witness, your attorney could review the questions ahead of time with the witness. This way, the witness

has time to formulate a thoughtful, clear answer. Most people are nervous about giving recorded testimony. Reviewing the questions ahead of time with the witness can reduce the witness's anxiety and help the witness look more credible.

2. A deposition occurs in a controlled environment, usually in an office or a conference room, as opposed to a courtroom. The questioning at a deposition is generally more relaxed and less stressful for a witness.

3. The witness may avoid the cost and inconvenience of traveling to another state for the trial by giving his or her testimony in a local deposition. This can make for a happier witness who is more likely to give helpful testimony.

The Disadvantages of Video Depositions

Keep in mind that there are also drawbacks to video depositions, such as these:

1. With a deposition, you lose some of the persuasive effect or emotional impact of live testimony. Watching a person on a video screen is much different from seeing the same person a few feet away on the witness stand.

2. The demeanor of a person may be different in a video deposition. Depending on which side you are on, this may help you or hurt you.

3. With a deposition, you cannot ask follow-up questions after the video has played in court. If the judge has additional questions, that could be an issue. Similarly, if any significant developments have occurred since the deposition, you will not be able to explore the impact of those new facts with the witness. Sometimes a judge will allow a phone call to the witness in open court, on the record, for follow-up questions. This is rare, though, and questions and answers over the phone can be confusing and difficult to follow.

4. Even when they are less expensive than live witnesses, depositions can still be very costly. You may need to have the video deposition transcribed into written form for the court's records. Further, the lawyers are paid for their time at a deposition, and depositions tend to take at least several hours. And, of course, you'll have to pay the additional costs to travel to the state where the witness resides. Sometimes attorneys retain a local attorney to conduct the deposition to reduce costs. In the long run, this is sometimes more costly, given the time required to get the local attorney up to speed on your case.

Remember that depositions are binding sworn testimony. Once the deposition is complete, a party can enter that testimony into evidence.

Can the Other Side Object to My Use of a Video Deposition?

If the other side cannot afford to be present at the deposition, the other lawyer could file a motion to quash the deposition. If the court quashes the deposition, it may not allow the party to play the video in court or may not allow the deposition to happen at all. The other lawyer could allege that it would be unfair to allow the deposition given the financial strain that it would impose on that party. The attorney could also allege that the opposing party is conducting the deposition primarily to harass the witness, if valid reasons support this argument. As with everything in the law, the court's decision will depend on the particular facts of each situation.

Can I Require Witnesses to Appear Even If They Live Several States Away?

Parties may subpoena out-of-state witnesses to court if they follow the proper procedures. Even with correct procedures, though, witnesses may still object to appearing in court due to the distance or cost involved. In that case, it would be up to the judge to decide whether the witnesses actually have to appear.

If a witness objects to coming to court, you can ask the court to require the witness to appear. First, though, give some thought to whether that's a good idea. Compelling an appearance over an objection usually gets you an angry witness, and that may not be the witness you want on the stand. In some situations, it may be necessary to require a witness to appear regardless of his or her feelings about testifying in court.

How Do I Present Out-of-State Records to the Court?

It's a common misconception that you can present any information in written form as evidence in court. This is not so. Every record that you offer into evidence in court must be authenticated by either the person who prepared the document or the document's custodian (the person who has the document).

Just like it sounds, *authentication* ensures that the documents that parties use in court are authentic—not fabricated, forged, or modified.

Let's say, for example, that you moved with your child to another state and enrolled your child in school before your court hearing. You have the teacher's notes about how well your child is doing in school. You want to enter them into evidence so the court knows that this move has benefited your child. How can you authenticate those notes?

The teacher could come to court to testify that he or she prepared the notes, but that isn't likely to happen.

The other party could agree that the notes are legitimate and consent to entering them without the teacher being present.

Alternatively, you could depose the teacher and present the notes during the deposition. You would need the teacher to read from those notes or summarize their contents. Later, at the hearing, you could show the teacher's deposition in court, if the judge allows it.

What about medical records? You can enter those into evidence without the doctor coming to court, right? Wrong. The doctor must be in court to testify that the records are the real deal. Otherwise, you can depose the doctor and elicit testimony about the records in the deposition.

Self-Authenticating Records

Thankfully, some records *self-authenticate*. You can enter these records into evidence without a witness verifying their authenticity. Self-authenticating records include the following:

- public documents under seal;
- certified copies of public records;
- official publications that a public authority issued, such as books, pamphlets, or other publications; and
- newspapers and periodicals.

These are just a few of the types of documents that are self-authenticating. How can any of these records be helpful? For example, let's say an article in the local paper publishes a glowing report about the school that you plan for your child to attend in your new state. The paper claims that this is one of the best schools anywhere. You could offer this article into evidence when you discuss where your child would attend school.

How Do I Subpoena Records or Witnesses in Another State?

First, what is a *subpoena*? A subpoena is a method that a party uses to request that certain documents or witnesses be produced in court or at a deposition.

Issuing a subpoena in North Carolina to request the appearance in court of documents or a witness is fairly easy. Your attorney completes the subpoena form and has it *served* on the custodian of the documents or on the witness, in accordance with the state's legal service requirements.

A subpoena must be served properly to be effective. Typically, parties can serve subpoenas by certified mail, or a police officer or a third-party process server can deliver them. If one of these official methods is not used—if you, a family member, a friend, or your attorney just leaves a subpoena on someone's doorstep—it isn't valid service.

The person subpoenaed to appear in court or to produce documents has the right to object to the subpoena if valid grounds exist for an objection. The judge must hear those objections and then determine whether to allow the subpoena or quash it.

If the witness or document you need is located in another state, the subpoena process is more complicated. You must follow that state's rules regarding subpoenas. If your case is in North Carolina, you may also have to obtain a *commission* for the subpoena. That commission simply authorizes you to conduct a deposition and swear the necessary oaths in another state on behalf of your North Carolina case.

Why does this matter? Out-of-state subpoenas increase the cost of your case and may waste valuable time. Dealing with objections from a person you have subpoenaed is also expensive and time-consuming.

You may ask your attorney to issue subpoenas in another state anyway, but be prepared for potential objections and substantial costs.

But Really: How Does It Work When I Need Out-of-State Records and Witnesses?

In most of these cases, the majority of the in-court testimony comes from the two parents and any family members who are willing to travel. More often than not, teachers and doctors are not present at these hearings.

Brainstorm to come up with lower-cost options that may help you establish the same points with the court.

- Instead of presenting a teacher's notes, you may find an article in the newspaper describing the school.

- Rather than the teacher testifying, you may testify about your visits at the school and the advantages that the school has to offer for your children.

- Instead of the gymnastics coach testifying about the extracurricular program offered in your new location, you may bring a publicly distributed brochure describing the program.

Often, lower-cost alternatives can help you prove your essential facts to the court. Your attorney can guide you in how to use other forms of evidence when you cannot present certain witnesses and documents in court.

Nonetheless, if a witness or document is truly critical to your case, you may have no choice but to incur the costs and have the witness or documents produced in court. Talk with your attorney about the best course of action to pursue.

WHO PAYS FOR
TRAVEL EXPENSES WHEN
A PARENT MOVES WITH A CHILD?

The court has allowed your ex-wife to move to New Jersey with your three-year-old son. You still live in North Carolina. The court has awarded you visits every other weekend, on half of the major holidays, and over the entire summer. But visiting with your son just became much more difficult, especially because he is so young. You are beyond frustrated with the increase in travel time and the substantial cost involved with seeing your son.

Do you have to bear all those costs yourself? Can you make the party who wanted to move away pay for your visits or at least share the costs? If you have a child support order, you can ask the court to factor travel expenses for visitation into that order.

What Are Travel Expenses?

Travel expenses may include airfare, train or bus fare, gas, hotels, and sometimes meals. The list of travel expenses can be extensive, depending on the facts of your case.

The key is showing the court how your expenses directly relate to the travel necessary to see your child.

Typically, a meal on a weekend with your child would not be considered a travel expense. This would be an ordinary expense for a parent.

However, it may be that you would usually eat at home, but the type of travel required to see your child results in you eating out significantly more. In that case, you should present the expense to the

NORTH CAROLINA CHILD RELOCATION LAW

court for consideration as an additional travel expense associated with your child custody and visitation schedule.

Travel Expenses That Could Be Associated With the Above Custody Schedule

Plane tickets are already expensive, but scheduling a flight for a minor adds even more fees and costs. The first issue you face is that your child is under five years old. Most airlines will not allow a child that age to fly alone. Even then, the child may only be allowed to take direct flights unaccompanied until he is significantly older.

Typically, airlines charge extra fees, ranging from $50 to $150 or more, both ways, for a child to fly alone.

So, if you need to use air travel to see your child, you would have to fly with the child. In other words, if you wanted to have the visitation in your own home, you would have to fly to New Jersey, retrieve your child, and fly back to North Carolina. That seems crazy, right?

The other option is flying up to New Jersey, paying for a hotel, and visiting there, eating out the whole time. Either way, these options are less than ideal. The costs add up fast. What used to be a $50 weekend with your son now is easily a $1,000 weekend.

Of course, you love your son, and you want to spend as much time as you can with him. But let's be real. Your income cannot support an extra $1,000 to $2,000 a month in visitation expenses associated with travel.

Maybe the train would be cheaper?

Trains go up and down the East Coast daily, but the trip from North Carolina to New Jersey is easily eight hours. You may have to take time off from work to have your son for the weekend, which would cut into your income. The time you spend on the train could also reduce your time with your son.

As with flying, your son has to be at least 12 to ride the train alone.

That won't be an option for years to come.

The visitation would have to take place in New Jersey. Otherwise, you would spend your entire weekend with your son riding the train down to North Carolina and then back to New Jersey. Visits in New Jersey demand that you get a hotel for the weekend.

Driving is always an option if all else fails, right?

You could always drive to visit your son, but that's hardly better. It would cost at least a few hundred dollars in gas, round trip, not to mention the wear and tear on your vehicle. Driving could take as long as 10 hours one way, so again you would have to get a hotel for the weekend. How could you even make this drive for just a weekend visit?

Whether you go by plane, train, or automobile, your visitation costs have now doubled or even tripled, thanks to the court's ruling. What in the world can you do? Is there any relief from the extra costs?

Ask the Court to Give You Credit for Travel Expenses

Travel expenses related to visitation, such as the costs discussed above, are addressed in the context of child support. These expenses are not automatically awarded simply because a parent is allowed to move a child out of state, thereby increasing the other parent's travel expenses for visitation.

The North Carolina Child Support Guidelines consider travel costs extraordinary expenses. You have to file a motion to modify child support to address your travel-related expenses. You can file that request either in your response to the motion to modify custody or later in a separate motion.

Extraordinary expenses are a line item on the child support worksheet. The court will insert the sum it deems appropriate for travel expenses to factor into the child support calculation.

In some scenarios, a motion to deviate from the North Carolina Child Support Guidelines might be appropriate. If the expenses are too great and the resulting credit on the child support worksheet doesn't create a fair distribution of expenses, or if other factors in the case warrant an exception, you could file a motion for a deviation.

What Do I Present to the Court as Evidence of My Travel Expenses?

The type of evidence that you present will depend on the mode of transportation you choose for visitation.

If you decide that flying is truly the most effective option, then the court needs to see all the expenses associated with flying. If you have previous receipts and records of prior flights, you can share them with the court. Bring the court reasonable estimates of the costs that you expect to incur if the visitation schedule is just beginning and you have no history of expenses.

Expenses for flying would include, at a minimum, the flight cost, fees for checking a bag, parking at the airport, ground transportation, and so on. Each case will be different, so it is critical to think through every expense you might incur. Your attorney can assist you with obtaining the best documentation to establish these expenses.

Another factor to consider is the child's age. If your child is older, you may have different expenses. For instance, a 10-year-old on a flight by himself may want to use his iPad to watch movies. A reasonable extra expense might be buying internet service for him to use during the flight.

You can testify to the court about the expenses you expect to incur for visitation. The court needs to hear from you to understand your side of this, so be prepared with detailed information.

For example, testifying that it will "probably" be expensive to fly your child from New Jersey to North Carolina will not assist the court. It is far better to say, "Flying my son from New Jersey to North Carolina to visit with me will cost around $400 in flights for both of us. It will also cost $15 in parking and $50 in gas since the airport is 40 miles from my home."

The reality is that some of your expenses will be estimates for the court to consider unless you already have actual receipts detailing expenses. Therefore, your informed testimony about the expenses is essential for the court to hear.

Don't Forget to Consider
Hidden or Unexpected Expenses

Just when you think you have all of your bases covered, you discover yet another cost associated with visits.

Don't miss out on telling the court about all of your costs. Take the time to think through every expense that might pop up.

Consider the following:

- the cost of gas to drive to and from the airport, if it is more than a few miles from your home, or the cost of a cab or other ground transportation;

- parking fees at the airport;

- fees for checked bags at the airport;

- increased car maintenance costs if you are driving significantly more due to the move;

- hotel or lodging expenses for your visits, including tips and fees;

- a significant increase in the cost of meals due to traveling; and

- any impact on your income due to the increased travel.

Does the Court Have to Give Parents Credit for Their Travel Expenses?

No. Under the North Carolina Child Support Guidelines, expenses incurred to transport children between the parents' homes are extraordinary expenses that the court *may* consider in calculating child support.

If a party claims to have incurred or expects to incur travel expenses associated with visitation, the trial court is not required to give that parent any credit.

The trial court has the discretion to decide whether, how, and to what extent it should credit travel expenses. Each case will be unique, decided on its own specific set of facts and circumstances.

The most important point to remember is that you must come prepared, ready to discuss in detail the expenses you have incurred or expect to incur. Provide as much documentation as possible to support your figures.

Real-Life Examples of the Court Giving Credit for Travel Expenses

There are two scenarios to examine:

1. a parent has a history of travel expenses, or
2. a parent will now be incurring new travel expenses because the court modified the custody order.

Sometimes, you'll have a history of actual travel expenses you incurred before the matter is heard in court. This certainly makes it easier to show how much you have spent or will spend going forward. Where you have actual receipts and current proof of expenses, the court does not have to engage in guesswork to calculate any credit.

However, most times you will not have a history of expenses, so you will have to testify about your expected expenses.

EXAMPLE 1: Child Support Adjusted for Travel Expenses

Eli and Erica have two children. Erica has primary custody, and Eli has visitation rights. Erica moved to Georgia, while Eli stayed in North Carolina. The parties agreed to the move but have not yet requested a modification of the custody order.

Each party has now filed motions to modify child support and child custody to reflect the new custody arrangement. Eli alleges that he has already spent significant sums on travel for visitation.

Eli testified and presented evidence at the hearing to support his costs. He demonstrated that he spent, on average, $300 to $500 monthly in visitation-related expenses and another $125 per month for the children's airfare.

The trial court's custody order contemplates visitation between Eli and his minor children in both North Carolina and Georgia. The court gave Eli credit for $300 per month in travel expenses for visitation.

EXAMPLE 2: No Child Support Adjustment for Travel Expenses

Betty and Bill have joint physical custody of their children according to a consent custody order. Betty moved to California without seeking a modification of custody.

The children remained with Bill in North Carolina.

Over the course of two years, the children have visited Betty twice. Betty paid for those visitation expenses.

Both parents have now filed motions to modify custody.

At the hearing, Betty testified that she would spend, on average, $250 a month to have the children visit her in California. That monthly estimate was based on the total costs of the children visiting her three times each year.

The court modified the custody order to award Betty eight weeks of continuous visitation during the summer. Betty would not be required to pay child support during this eight-week period.

However, the court refused to adjust Betty's overall child support based on her estimated $250 monthly visitation expenses. In this case, the court seemed to be swayed by the fact that Betty had only paid for the children to visit her twice over the previous two years. The court also factored in the eight weeks of summer visitation when she would not pay child support.

Here, the history of travel expenses seemed to factor into the court's decision. The outcome may well have been different if Betty had paid for the children to visit her more than twice in a two-year period.

Expenses May Change Over Time

As children grow up, expenses associated with visitation may change. You may find, as the court above did with Betty, that it is more economical to have longer, less frequent visits with your children.

It's also possible that down the line, you may have to go to court again to revisit travel expenses and the visitation schedule.

What's the Bottom Line?

As with most child custody and support matters, the facts and circumstances of each case are unique, and decisions are made on a case-by-case basis.

It is critical that you prepare ahead of time. You must be ready to show the court what you have spent or will spend on travel expenses if a custody modification increases your travel expenses.

Discuss the matter thoroughly with your attorney so he or she can guide you on the type of evidence needed in your particular case.

HOW DO I CO-PARENT
WHEN MY KIDS LIVE IN ANOTHER STATE?

Now that you've gone through the legal process of modifying your custody order to accommodate a parent's relocation, you face the daunting task of long-distance co-parenting. It's hard enough to co-parent when your ex lives down the road or in the next town over. So how do you co-parent when your ex lives hours or states away from you?

Regardless of whether you're the parent relocating or the parent who is left behind, know that it is possible to successfully co-parent in a long-distance situation to the benefit of your kids. Here, we explore some of these ideas to help you transition smoothly into long-distance co-parenting.

What Can I Do If I'm the Parent Being Left Behind?

When your ex decided to relocate and take the kids to another state, you probably felt devastated, upset, and even angry. You've likely spent the last several years living near your kids. You picked them up after school a few days a week, attended their soccer games and piano recitals, and saw them on holidays and on their birthdays. You stayed up to date on their lives by attending parent-teacher conferences and doctor's appointments. Best of all, you've been able to simply hang out with them on the weekends when everyone is off from work and school.

But with your kids living far away from you, you won't be able to do any of these things without serious planning. Your new custody schedule might carve out a large block of time for you to see your kids, for example, a month or two in the summer. You're looking forward to having that quality time, but what do you do during the school year and during the week?

How Can I Stay Involved in My Kids' Lives?

Don't just throw in the towel. There are many ways to let your children know that, even though you're not physically nearby, you're still very interested in their lives. Consider these options:

- using FaceTime and/or Skype for video calls instead of regular telephone calls;

- exchanging text messages and emails;

- using online shared calendars with the other parent and the kids;

- talking to your children regularly, asking questions, hearing about their activities, and learning the names of the new people in their lives;

- watching the same TV shows or playing the same online game as your kids so you have a common activity—even if you can't actually do it together;

- helping virtually with homework; and

- sending care packages or cards in the mail during tough times or on special occasions.

Take Advantage of Technology

Today's advanced technology makes it easier than ever to stay in touch despite long distances. Your kids are using that technology to talk with their friends. You can stay connected with them this way too.

FaceTime and/or Skype

Many long-distance parents find FaceTime or Skype to be a helpful, enjoyable way to stay in touch with their children. Unlike regular telephone calls, FaceTime and Skype use cameras and video technology to let you and your kids see each other while you talk. iPhone users can make calls through FaceTime, which allows both sides of the call to see each other, using the phone's camera, as they talk. Skype uses the webcam on your computer to do the same thing.

With these features, not only can you talk to your children, but you can see them too, and they can see you.

Texts and Emails

For older children who have their own cell phones or their own email addresses, you can quickly and easily stay in touch with your children despite the distance between you. Texting and emailing are also great ways for you and your kids to share pictures.

Online Shared Calendars

Online calendars and scheduling websites and apps allow parents to share a calendar where they can keep up with their kids' activities and events.

If you and your co-parent can both agree to use such a website or app and to keep it current, you'll have an easy way to see what your kids are doing from day to day.

For example, if your child has a baseball game or a major test coming up, your co-parent can schedule it in the shared calendar where you can view it. When you next talk to your child, you'll know to ask how the game or the test went. You can even send a quick "good luck" text beforehand.

You can also schedule recurring phone calls or video calls on the shared calendar.

Maintain Consistency in Your Communications

One of the most important things you can do when your kids live in another state is to maintain regular, consistent communication with them.

Say you plan to talk with your kids on the phone or by FaceTime or Skype three times a week. Don't wait for a convenient time to come along; schedule those calls in advance. Set a specific day and time frame for when you will call: for example, you might agree to call every Monday, Wednesday, and Friday between 7:30 pm and 8:30 pm. Most importantly, follow through each and every time. Your court order or separation agreement may even specify what telephone contact is permitted.

Be sure that you initiate the communication when you say you will. Don't skip calls, and don't rely on your child to call you.

Ask Questions, Learn Names

When you do get to talk to your kids, whether it's by telephone or on video, be ready to ask them questions. You might ask your daughter about her day, how she did on a test, what she did with her friends over the weekend, how her soccer game went, etc.

Ask open-ended questions. Questions that your children can answer with a simple "yes" or "no" don't give you much real information or help you start a discussion.

Also, ask questions about specific people who are important in your kids' lives. Learn the names of your children's teachers, close friends, new babysitter, and so on. You might not know these people, but they matter to your children. Knowing who is involved in your children's daily lives will improve your connection with them.

Not only is asking questions important to help your kids feel more connected to you, but it also benefits you. Staying in tune with your kids' lives can make them feel closer, regardless of the physical distance between you.

Watch the Same TV and Play the Same Games

This may sound unusual, but watching TV or playing an online game can actually help you bond with your kids.

You and your child might agree ahead of time to watch the same TV show or sports game and discuss it afterward. Or you and your child can play the same online game at the same time.

So, even if you are many miles away from your kids, you can still connect with them, as if they were watching TV next to you or gaming just down the hall.

Help with Homework

Who says you have to be in the same room to help your children with their homework?

With today's technology, especially video services such as FaceTime and Skype, you can help your children with their homework even if you are in another state. Encourage your children to FaceTime or Skype you if they have a question about an assignment. You might establish "on call" hours on certain evenings when your kids can ask for homework help. Alternatively, you and your co-parent could divide your child's school subjects between you so your child knows who to ask for help with reading or math.

Also, many schools are using the internet for assignments and staying in touch with parents. Regularly log in to their school's internet portal to keep up with assignments and projects.

Send a Care Package

You know it's true: everyone loves getting a package in the mail, especially kids. And packages are even more exciting when you send them for no particular reason (as in, it's not their birthday or a holiday).

Every once in a while, send a package to your children with a few things they would enjoy or that might cheer them up.

Want to send a themed care package? Search online for ideas. Sites like Pinterest can be a rich source of inspiration.

And don't forget about a card in the mail every once in a while. Sending a simple card by regular mail can let your children know you're thinking about them even though you're not there.

What Can I Do If I'm the Parent Leaving and Taking the Kids With Me?

You've decided to relocate to another state, and your kids will be coming with you. Between packing, unpacking, learning your away around a new town, figuring out your new job, meeting new neighbors and friends, and getting your kids adjusted to new schools, you've got a lot on your mind. On top of that, you've got to figure out how to co-parent with your ex now that the two of you live miles or states apart.

You want your children to maintain their relationships with the other parent. Your kids are also probably upset not only about the upheaval in their lives but also about being so far away from their other parent.

How Can I Make Sure My Kids Stay Involved with their Other Parent?

Of course, you will make sure that your kids visit with their other parent according to your court order or written agreement. But you can do several other things to help your kids and your co-parent stay connected, such as these:

- Support your ex's attempts to stay connected with the kids.

- Encourage your kids to maintain regular contact with their other parent.

- Keep your co-parent updated about the events and goings-on in your kids' lives.

Be Supportive of Your Co-Parent

Arguably, the most important thing to do when you are the parent relocating with your children is to be supportive of the parent left behind. That means you should not only support your kids when they want to talk to or contact your ex, but you should also support your ex's efforts to stay connected with the kids.

Remember, your move with the children is tough on your ex. He or she has always been involved with your kids' daily lives. Now, all of a sudden, that regular contact is gone. Your co-parent is bound to miss the children as much as you would if your roles were reversed.

So, try to be accommodating when your ex says he or she wants to have regular FaceTime calls or telephone calls with your kids. Uphold your end of the deal by making sure that your kids are home and available during the scheduled time for those calls. If your children are younger or do not have their own cell phones, make sure you either have a landline or that your cell phone is charged, on, and not silenced so that you will hear the phone ring.

If your ex talks to your child about watching the same show or football game on TV, for example, let your child watch that show or game. Don't interfere with or undermine your ex's efforts—you'll only be hurting your kids in the long run.

Help Your Kids Stay in Touch

Not only should you support the efforts your ex makes to stay connected with the kids, but you should encourage your children to stay in contact as well.

Reminding them to talk with their other parent during a regularly scheduled call is a great start. But you should urge them to call or text your ex at other times too: when your child has an accomplishment to share, needs help with homework, or needs advice and support. You can encourage your child to reach out for no other reason than to simply say hello.

When your children are on the phone with their other parent, allow them to talk freely together. Don't constantly monitor the conversation. Also, never try to find out the details of your ex's life through your kids' conversations with him or her.

When your ex sends a care package or a card in the mail, give it to your kids right away. They'll be thrilled to receive something in the mail, so be excited with them when they open the box or envelope.

Share Your Kids' Schedule

Keep your co-parent up to date with all the events in your children's lives.

Use a shared calendar on an app or website and take the time to enter in each upcoming event. Just like you would want to know when your kids have a softball game, a gymnastics competition, a play date with a friend, or a major project due at school, so does the other parent. Since your ex can't attend these events like you can, at least help him or her keep up with what your kids are doing each day or week.

Sharing all the events in your children's lives will enable all of you—you, your children, and your co-parent—to stay better connected. With a shared calendar, your ex can ask about specific events when he or she talks to your kids. This helps your kids understand that even though distance separates them from their other parent, they have not lost their relationships with that parent.

With Some Effort, the Distance Won't Be So Great

With a little extra effort on the part of both parents, the long distance that separates the kids from one of their parents doesn't have to seem so daunting.

Long-distance parents can still effectively co-parent and stay involved in their kids' lives by taking advantage of technology and maintaining regular contact.

It won't always be easy. But when both parents put forth the additional effort, their children are the ones who benefit. Aim for your children to maintain or even strengthen the great parent-child relationships they had prior to your relocation.

HOW MUCH
IS A RELOCATION CASE GOING TO COST ME?

It's a common complaint. Attorneys are too expensive. What are all these fees for anyway? Shouldn't this process be more affordable?

We're not going to hide this: hiring an attorney to represent you in a custody trial is a costly endeavor. Good attorneys are not cheap. And the good ones will tell you that they are worth it. Most of the time they are, but that doesn't change the fact that it's expensive to fight custody in court with an attorney by your side.

Any custody battle is expensive, but a custody case involving a relocation is even more so. If some or all of the evidence may be in a state other than where the case will be heard, the fees can increase almost exponentially for a variety of reasons.

What Are the Typical Costs in a Custody Trial? How Do They Differ in Relocation Cases?

As with most legal trials, the costs can pile up. The following are common tasks your lawyer may need to do, each of which will add to your costs:

- preparing and responding to pleadings,
- drafting interrogatories,
- preparing requests for admissions,
- requesting production of documents,
- preparing for and conducting depositions,

- creating and filing subpoenas,

- preparing exhibits for trial,

- preparing witnesses for trial,

- consulting with and preparing expert witnesses, such as doctors, and

- preparing legal arguments.

Discovery is typically the most expensive trial cost. Discovery is the gathering of information to prepare your case for trial. Many of the tasks above relate to discovery methods in North Carolina.

The costs vary in each case, as every item above is not necessary in every case. It depends on what facts must be established and what methods are most effective for proving those facts.

Let's go through each of these items and examine how these costs may or may not increase in a relocation matter.

Pleadings

For any court case to begin, one party must file a lawsuit with the necessary allegations to start the ball rolling for a claim of custody. In a relocation matter, the pleading typically filed is the *motion to modify* an existing custody order. Also, complaints, answers, and responses are all types of pleadings that may need to be filed.

Pleadings in North Carolina are usually straightforward. They simply give a general outline of a party's contentions. Pleadings do not have to be pages and pages long.

Each party pays his or her own attorney to either prepare or respond to the other party's pleadings. Pleadings must be accurate, as the parties sign their pleadings under oath, asserting that their statements are true. Pleadings are a necessary part of all court matters, but they are not usually the most expensive part of your case.

This cost would not necessarily increase for relocation cases.

Interrogatories

Interrogatories are a useful discovery tool that allows parties to obtain baseline information such as past addresses, birthdates, past employers, and employer addresses. They are simply a set of questions that your attorney prepares and mails to opposing counsel. The other party has to answer all of those questions.

In North Carolina, you are limited to 50 interrogatories, restricting how much information you can gain by sending them. In most cases, you will get more information from a deposition than you will from interrogatories.

The answers to the interrogatories must be signed and verified, just like pleadings.

Interrogatories would not be more expensive in a relocation case.

Requests for Admissions

Requests for admissions, like interrogatories, are written questions mailed to the opposing counsel for the opposing party to answer. They ask the other party whether they admit to certain facts. For example, you might ask, "Do you admit or deny that you had an affair with your neighbor?" Unlike interrogatories, though, there is no limit to requests for admissions. You can send as many as you like.

You typically don't gain a tremendous amount of information from requests for admissions, because they are yes-no questions. However, they do force the opposing party to answer difficult questions or explain why they won't answer, which can be helpful.

If a party does not answer requests for admissions within the time frame allotted under the court's rules of civil procedure, then they are deemed to have admitted every allegation. If you had asked the question above in an alimony dispute, an admission would be quite useful. Requests for admissions are always worth doing in case the opposing party misses the deadline. It doesn't happen often, but attorneys—and more importantly, their clients—get lucky every now and then.

This cost mostly depends on the number of requests sent. Some attorneys use this discovery tool to bombard the other side, since numerous questions can take time to evaluate and answer. Writing or responding to extensive requests for admissions can drive up costs.

This cost would not be higher in a relocation case.

Requests for Production of Documents

A request to produce documents is very common in most family law cases. This discovery tool allows you to request any documents that you believe may have information pertinent to your case. If the opposing party has those documents, and if they contain relevant information, your opponent must produce them for you to review.

The primary expense associated with requesting and producing documents is the time needed for your attorney and his or her staff to review those documents and identify information that is pertinent to your case.

This would not be more expensive in a relocation case.

Depositions

At a deposition, a witness testifies under oath and answers questions from one or more attorneys. Depositions take place outside of court, but they are typically recorded. The video or transcript may be used later in court. The usual costs of depositions include time for the attorneys to ask questions and time for the court reporter to record or transcribe the questions and answers.

If an important witness resides in the state you would like to move to and you need to depose this person, expect that it will cost more than a typical in-state deposition. In most cases, an out-of-state witness could not be compelled to come to North Carolina for a North Carolina case. The deposition must be conducted in his or her state. You'll have to follow the appropriate rules for out-of-state depositions.

Your in-state attorney may need to engage an out-of-state attorney, someone local to the witness, to conduct the deposition. This would drive up costs because you are employing another attorney. In the alternative, your attorney could travel to the state where the witness resides and take the deposition directly. This too could prove costly.

So, for example, a single in-state deposition can easily cost more than $2,000 when you factor in your attorney's time and the costs of the court reporter. Now, add out-of-state travel expenses or employing an attorney in another state, and you've easily doubled your costs.

This cost could double for a relocation case. To keep your costs from skyrocketing, you will want to depose only the witnesses you truly need to prove your case.

Subpoenas

Subpoenas are used to compel persons to appear in court or at a deposition or to produce documents. The average cost to serve a subpoena in North Carolina is less than $200.

To serve a subpoena to an out-of-state person or entity would likely be several hundred dollars because you'll have to follow additional processes. You would probably engage an attorney in the state where the subpoena is to be served to assist you with serving the subpoena according to the laws of that state.

Subpoenas will cost more in a relocation case, but your attorney would probably not send many out-of-state subpoenas unless they were truly necessary.

Preparation of Exhibits for Trial

Exhibits can be anything that you want the judge to look at or consider during your trial other than live testimony. Exhibits that might be used in a custody trial include the following:

- pictures of the home where the child will live, including the child's bedroom;

- copies of the child's report cards, if any;

- custodial evaluations, if any were performed;

- deposition transcripts for out-of-state witnesses;

- text messages sent between parties;

- emails sent between parties; and

- Facebook and other social media postings that were legally obtained.

The attorneys offer exhibits for the court's consideration. The judge ultimately decides which exhibits to admit into evidence.

You'll incur costs as your attorney and his or her staff obtain, prepare, and label exhibits for trial. These costs include making copies of exhibits to distribute to the judge and to opposing counsel. Most attorneys will assemble an exhibit notebook to ensure that each exhibit is presented to the court at the right time and none is overlooked as the trial progresses. Court can be fast moving, so your attorney must be prepared and keep track of your exhibits.

For the most part, this cost would not be any higher in a relocation case than in any other case.

Witness Preparation

Witness preparation is critical in every type of case. Your attorney needs to know, as well as can be known, what testimony your witnesses will give. There is always a measure of unpredictability with witnesses, because you cannot know for certain what questions the opposing counsel may ask the witness.

Your attorney's goal in preparation is to ask potential witnesses as many questions as possible so you know how they will help—or hurt—your case. This takes time, and time costs money.

If you're calling witnesses at trial to testify on your behalf, it's because you believe their testimony will benefit you. In reality, if your witnesses are coming from out of state, they are coming voluntarily, because they want to help you. You would therefore not incur any additional costs associated with their appearance in court.

The cost of witness preparation in a relocation case should be similar to the cost in any other case.

Expert Witness Consultation and Preparation

If you need experts to testify in your case, your costs will go up. First, you have to pay the expert witness for his or her time in court. You also must prepare that expert ahead of time to be sure your attorney fully understands the expert's testimony and its impact on your case. In many cases, the opposing party will also want to depose your expert witness before the trial. Once your opponent gets a sense of what your expert might say, he or she may then seek out another expert to counter that opinion. All of these appearances take time and cost money.

Let's consider an example. Say that your son has bad asthma. You take him to a doctor you know well and trust completely. Your ex-husband doesn't know that doctor and believes that you are exaggerating your son's condition. He contests the issue because your son's medicine and treatments cost at least a few hundred dollars each month. Your ex-husband decides to take your child to another doctor for a second opinion.

Not only did you have to depose your own doctor, but now you may also have to depose the new doctor. Your husband also wants to depose your doctor. You've gone from one doctor to two and doubled the deposition costs. See how quickly your costs can increase?

In good news, you generally won't use experts in custody cases. They're only necessary in certain circumstances.

But say, for example, that you've relocated to another state with your asthmatic son. Your doctor is in the state where you want to move rather than the state of your trial. Your expert costs can easily double again because of the distance.

If your relocation case demands an expert witness, expect a significant cost increase.

Legal Argument Preparation

Your witnesses aren't the only ones who have to be prepared for trial! Your attorney will also need to invest time in preparing the arguments he or she will use in court. Remember that each case is different— your attorney will want to take enough time to assess your case and develop its strengths while minimizing its weaknesses.

This doesn't cost more for a relocation case than for any other case, although more complicated cases tend to be more expensive.

So How Much More Does a Relocation Case Cost?

Depending on the case, your costs could increase exponentially or not much at all.

In many cases, much of the evidence will be testimony from the parties. You may not need any depositions or subpoenas.

For example, a recent relocation case we handled in Orange County, North Carolina, cost the same as a standard custody case with no relocation issues. No depositions were needed to prepare this particular case, and there were only a few subpoenas. There were no out-of-state witnesses. The case testimony was primarily from the parties themselves and a few relatives.

Keep in mind that it is impossible to accurately predict the total costs of any custody case; they all have the potential for unexpected twists and turns that can suddenly complicate matters. For example, you thought your ex was a fairly good dad until a friend told you that he now abuses prescription pills. You and your attorney believe you must make a motion to the court for a hair follicle drug test, followed by random drug screens for at least a few months if the follicle test is positive. That motion was not a cost that you anticipated at the outset. This is just one example of how costs in custody cases can increase quickly and without warning.

What Can You Do to Control Costs?

Good news: there are several things you can do to keep your costs down in your case. The common theme is that you want to help your attorney help you!

Keep Notes and Be Organized

Keeping a thorough calendar and a notebook documenting day-to-day events related to your custody case is very helpful to your attorney. It can also help you remember important information as time passes.

Ask your attorney whether he or she prefers any particular format for your notes or whether there is a calendar that he or she finds especially useful.

When you meet with your attorney, bring all of your notes and papers. Have them organized and make sure they are easy to read so that your attorney doesn't have to spend a lot of time interpreting your scribbled notes. Highlight important points to quickly draw attention to them.

Instead of calling your attorney five times in one day because new ideas keep popping into your head, write down each question or issue as it comes up and make one call. Of course, if it's an emergency, call right away. But for day-to-day events and questions, keep a running list and call once to save your attorney's time and your money. Alternatively, your attorney might prefer that you send one concise email.

Realize that custody cases are usually emotionally and physically draining. You are not the first person to experience a flood of emotions and thoughts. You may feel compelled to call or email your attorney each time your emotions kick in. While this is normal, just remember that your costs will add up if you call several times a day. Consolidating your questions in one call or email is a favor you can do for yourself.

From time to time, you may need to meet with your attorney to discuss events. Sometimes a call or email just won't suffice. If you schedule a meeting, come prepared to discuss the issues coherently and in a logical order.

Organize Your Printed Documents

Many custody cases include voluminous emails, Facebook posts, bank records, and so forth. When you provide these to your attorney, don't simply throw the whole disorganized pile in a box and hope he or she can make some sense of it.

Yes, it's tedious and unpleasant to sort through the papers that document the demise of your relationship. But if you make your attorney organize them, you'll be the one paying for it.

Do the Legwork When You Can

Say, for example, that you want a subpoena served on your ex's aunt to have her testify on your behalf at trial. Instead of making your attorney search for the address, do the legwork yourself. Find out and provide the aunt's complete legal name and her address if possible. There may not be much you can assist with in certain cases, but if you can help, do it!

Don't Hide Information from Your Lawyer

Custody cases often involve embarrassing information. It's just the nature of the beast. Personal information that you'd rather keep private always gets thrown in the mix. Some of it is relevant, but some of it isn't.

Tell your attorney anything you feel might be relevant to your case. Answer all questions truthfully, even when you don't like your own answers. Hiding information that could come out later will not help you. Not only can it increase your costs, but it might also cause you to lose your case completely.

So What's the Bottom Line?

In most relocation cases, only one party wants to move, and no one has actually left town yet. Much of the evidence may revolve around the party who is trying to move away. That parent will have to testify about all the benefits that the move would produce for the child, such as better schools, a safer neighborhood, more access to family, and so forth. Alternatively, the party contesting the move might discuss all the benefits the child has in the current state and how a move would strip those advantages away while reducing time with that parent.

In that common situation, a relocation case will not cost any more than any other custody case. Of course, as we have said many times before, every case is different, and your costs will depend on the facts of your particular case.

MOVING FORWARD

Your head is spinning. This is all too much! Why does this have to be so hard? Why does sharing a child with someone mean that he or she can at times completely control your life? It is certainly a harsh reality to accept: two households, one child. And what if you didn't even want to separate from the other parent at all? He or she wanted to leave the relationship, not you!

Sometimes people ask themselves, why am I even bothering with this move? This takes too much time, costs too much, and creates too much stress for myself and my child.

At times, relocation with a child seems like an impossible pursuit, but know that it does happen, and it can happen for you if you set up the right circumstances.

What you should know is that if you want to move with your children on a whim, for your own exclusive benefit, or for a temporary purpose, you aren't likely to succeed if the other parent opposes the move.

Few judges are going to allow you to uproot your children because you've taken up surfing and you think Hawaii sounds like a cool place to live. You need legitimate reasons to move, and the move must benefit your children.

Take some time to get "real" with your situation. Ask yourself these five questions:

1. What are the real reasons I want to move?
2. How important is this move?

3. What are the advantages and disadvantages to my children?

4. Is this move temporary or permanent?

5. How could I continue to foster a relationship between my children and the parent they will be leaving behind?

If you can't honestly answer these questions and feel good about this move for your children, you may want to stop there and put the idea of moving aside for a while.

But if you decide that you have legitimate answers to all of these questions, then start preparing yourself for trial. Put in the effort to carefully choose an attorney and thoroughly develop your case with him or her.

It's critical that you hire an attorney who has historical knowledge of how each judge in your district typically rules in relocation cases. Your attorney should also be experienced in actually trying these types of cases. That experience allows for effective and efficient preparation, which maximizes your chance of success.

Make no mistake: relocation cases can be complicated for everyone. A major move to another state, or even several hundred miles away within the same state, poses substantial challenges to the parent/child relationship. Living far away obviously reduces the physical time that one parent has with the children. Yes, Skype and FaceTime allow for more meaningful contact than phone calls, but video calls aren't the same as living five minutes away. You must develop a plan with your attorney for how you can facilitate a true and meaningful relationship between your children and the other parent. You must be willing to do that with no questions asked, for the sake of your children.

If you're the one moving, never forget that you're leaving a parent behind. That is always a big deal. Your demeanor should reflect your sensitivity to this issue whenever you are in court.

Surely, some situations are easier than others. For example, your co-parent may only see his child once a month at best, often skipping his visitation time completely. This scenario is much different from a situation where both parents share custody equally, alternating weeks, until the father wants to move out of state with the children for a new job.

When parents cannot agree, decisions regarding children will always be left in the hands of a judge. Always remember this: court is a gamble, and your odds of winning are rarely better than 50/50. Attorneys cannot guarantee an outcome; they can only represent you to the best of their ability.

The goal of this book was to open up a dialogue about relocation and the types of child custody issues that you can expect if you or your co-parent try to relocate.

If you understand your options and recognize the difficulties you may face, you will be well positioned to realistically evaluate your situation and make reasonable decisions.

We hope this book helped you and your family. If you have any questions, please don't hesitate to get in touch.

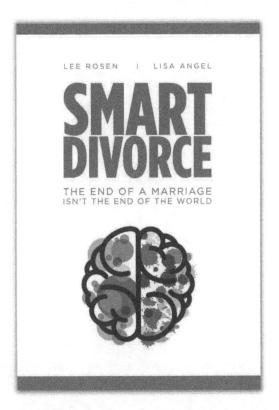